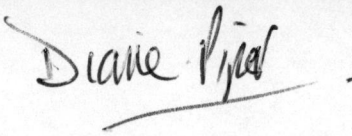

A Hermetic Path to the Stars

Journeys of discovery in hermetic astrology

JANET SAUNDERS

Hermes Books

First published 2018 by Hermes Books, Edinburgh

ISBN: 978-0-9927233-5-4

Printed in the UK by Bell & Bain Ltd., Glasgow

The paper used in this book is recyclable. It is made from low chlorine pulps produced in a low energy, low emissions manner from renewable forests.

Typeset by Main Point Books, Edinburgh
www.mainpointbooks.co.uk

Contents

Preface

In 1982 I was working in London in a busy housing office. I was resolutely atheist, political and radical. I was also intrigued by astrology, Jung's ideas on individuation and Gurdjieff. At this point in my life I suddenly lost my voice. I was not really ill, I just could not speak or work. I went home to Mum.

We visited a favourite town with a favourite bookshop, where I bought three books; the *Koran*, signalling my mystical fascination; the *I-Ching*, feeding my interest in divination and a book called *The Snow Leopard*, the story of Peter Matthiessen's physical and spiritual journey into the Himalaya. Out of this experience, the outer world I had created for myself caved in. It appeared a mere surface gloss over a deeper reality, which was compelling, alarming in its absolute demands, mysterious and personal. I realised I could not really get well unless I plunged into this deeper reality.

It felt necessary to bring together the three strands I was following: astrology, individuation and the mystical. I have pursued all three at different times, weaving in other strands such as shamanism, hypnotherapy, neuroscience and child and adult development. However, the strands had always retained their separation – until now.

In Part 1 of this book the threads are brought together. According to the hermetic sources, the cosmos is a living sacred being, mixed out of body, soul and spirit. The human has a special place in it, due to our paradoxical human nature and the soul's mediating role. On the one hand we are able, through reason, to negotiate our way through the material world, and on the other, through nous, or the higher mind, we have qualities of imagination and intuition and so are able to appreciate love and beauty as intrinsic to the spiritual life of the cosmos. The qualities of nous can be cultivated via reverence and intuition, and enable man to see the world symbolically and so divine the best course of action, in line with God's will. The recovery of these hermetic ideas in the Renaissance by the scholar Marsilio Ficino was central to his spiritual work and astrological practice. I have sought to draw out the hermetic threads and show how they inform Ficino's astrological hermeticism. These same threads can then be seen to run through the work of psychoanalyst C.G. Jung, soft systems thinker Jake Chapman and psychiatrist Iain McGilchrist to the present day.

Part 2, Journeys of Discovery, describes the story of the making of the play *The Journey of the Soul* and the drawing together of a variety of mystical ideas in its making.

Part 3 contains the script of the play, which offers an experiential approach to the hermetic creation story. Here the soul descends into the world, taking on divine qualities from the planetary daemons. This is followed by the soul's struggle to integrate these qualities consciously, ready for the return.

It is not necessary to read each part of this book in sequence. Feel free to start with Part 2 or 3 if you prefer.

Janet Saunders
March 2018

Acknowledgements

This book contains work produced as part of the MA in Myth, Cosmology and the Sacred at Canterbury Christchurch University. The course gave me the space, resources and encouragement to explore the hermetic roots of astrology, mysticism and human development. Developing these themes would not have been possible without the support of Angela Voss, Geoffrey Cornelius and Wilma Fraser. Their depth and range of knowledge, generously shared with their students, have been both humbling and inspiring. Their commitment to making the MA a course of philosophy in the original and initiatic sense has had an enlivening effect on all their students. (For a wide range of papers connected to the MA in Myth, Cosmology and the Sacred, see www.gnosticacademy.com.)

Many others have supported me through the study process. My fellow students gamely took on roles in the performance of the play, entering into the spirit of the thing with a verve that brought it to life. In Edinburgh many people commented on drafts, attended talks or helped me with rehearsals offering constructive feedback. Thanks must also go to Beryl and Graham Fellows for good humoured proofing, to Jennie Renton for typesetting and to Eric, Clare and Geoffrey Saunders for supporting me through it all.

Part 1

Hermeticism and astrology:
What is the relevance of hermetic astrology
for modern man?

Chapter 1

Engaging with the Hermetic Sources

*The love of God, unutterable and perfect, flows into a pure soul the
way that light rushes into a transparent object. The more love that it
finds, the more it gives itself; so that, as we grow clear and open, the
more complete the joy of heaven is. And the more souls who resonate
together, the greater the intensity of their love, and, mirror-like, each
soul reflects the other.*
Dante, *Purgatorio XV. 67–75*

In this book I set out key themes that are characteristic of
hermeticism. These themes in philosophy and practice can be
traced back to the world of Plato and the Platonic Academy and
forward in time to Arabic learning, and then into Europe, where
they were revivified by Marsilio Ficino in 15th century Florence.
Hermeticism continues to be an undercurrent in esotericism in
Europe to the present day.

I am a practising astrologer and would like to think about my
practice within a wider philosophical context, relevant to today,
yet drawing on deep roots in the western esoteric tradition. In
a more personal sense, I have long suspected that astrology has
both a mystical dimension and a role in human development.
I want to take this opportunity to try to weave these threads
together, since this has always felt so deeply meaningful to me. I
want to follow up the little play I wrote and performed, as part
of my MA in Myth, Cosmology and the Sacred at Canterbury
Christ Church University. For this I drew on mystical texts from

Rumi and Ibn 'Arabi, from the ideas of Ficino but most of all from the hermetic texts. The play brought the ideas in these texts to life in striking fashion. The writing of the play obliged me to focus on the source texts, fragmentary and sometimes confusing and obscure as they are. The texts contain ideas and images that are vivid, evocative and sometimes shocking. It is no wonder they have held an abiding fascination throughout the history of Western esotericism.

Approach to the subject

At no point does this book attempt to validate astrology as a predictive craft. The main themes in hermeticism are explored in Chapter 2 where astrology has a place amongst divinatory oracle practices. In Chapter 3 the hermetic themes are explored in the thoughts and astrological practice of Marsilio Ficino. In chapter 4 the hermetic themes are brought up to date with reference to the work of Iain McGilchrist on neuroscience, Professor Jake Chapman on soft systems thinking and of C.G. Jung on the unconscious, leading to some concluding thoughts on the possibility of a hermetic approach to astrological practice in the twenty-first century.

The status of astrologers is at a nadir in our times, yet Crystal Addey, in her talk,[1] told us how in classical times the status of astrologers and that of philosophers were on a par, mutually respectful and supportive. This is because the ancient world had a broader sense of the sources of knowledge; there were different ways of knowing. In this context all forms of divination, including astrology, could bring divine knowledge. Divination was not predictive, but rather a way of enabling people to look deeply into the present and explore viable scenarios for action and likely outcomes in a complex world.

The idea of paradox is a thread that runs throughout the *Corpus Hermeticum*[2] that seeks a path to dialectical resolution through the life of soul in the world, uniting body with spirit. In a parallel vein,

Iain McGilchrist[3] identifies the two hemispheres of the human brain as bringing into presence two world views, complementary, yet with different roles, that we constantly need to bring into relationship. There is a particularly intriguing correlation between McGilchrist's work and the *Corpus Hermeticum* when the latter speaks of nous and reason,[4] suggesting that its authors intuitively grasped this aspect of the paradoxical human.

For Ficino our dual nature informs both science and art. He works all the time with his own chart and those of his companions, and is constantly urging them to beware or take advantage, as appropriate, of the perceived relations of the planets in their observed positions in the sky. In this sense, he works with fate. However, he allows the planetary symbols their multivalence, extending their meanings to divine gifts and seeking to assimilate the divine intentions into himself and in this sense sets himself free.[5] He affirms that this depends on the judgement or *notio* of the astrologer; something that must combine a lifetime's practice of technique alongside a kind of daily theurgic self-purification.[6]

In our time, there is no presumption of the reality of soul and spirit. As Nietzsche says, God is dead, and so we are left with only dead matter on our hands. C.G. Jung[7] and James Hillman, along with the therapists working in the Transpersonal and Archetypal traditions, have sought to return soul to the world. Like the hermetic teachings, they give an ontological priority to psyche or soul. For Jung, psyche is our reality and many astrologers seek the image of psyche at the centre of the astrological chart. From this perspective we are always at the centre of our field of consciousness. From the hermetic perspective or that of McGilchrist, an objective validity for astrology is a requirement of the left hemisphere, of the "people of reason".[8] Its subjective value depends upon its healing power. Testimony to this can be found when therapists and astrologers work in parallel with their client as described by Delia Shargel.[9]

To enquire into the paradoxical nature of the human and propose a dialectical reconciliation has consequences for the enquirer and the enquiry. This study follows the position proposed by Arthur Versluis, who argues that "a sympathetic empiricist perspective may well be indispensable for understanding the work one is investigating". He is here "referring to an intermediate position that incorporates the best of both emic and etic approaches… scholarship that strives to achieve a standard of objectivity, and on the other hand the virtues of an approach that seeks to sympathetically understand one's subject, to understand it from the inside out, so to speak".[10] Versluis proposes that "Western esotericism … could perhaps best be characterized as a long series of different investigations into the nature of consciousness itself".[11] This matter of consciousness is a major theme of this study running from Ancient Greece and Egypt up to the present day. As Versluis says "one finds a consistently recurrent theme of transmuting consciousness, which is to say, of awakening latent, profound connections between humanity, nature, and the divine, and of restoring a paradisal union between them".[12] The twin approaches set out by Versluis are an apt parallel to the topic under discussion. The hermetic texts, Ficino and McGilchrist all distinguish a clear role for both focused study on the one hand and the sense of higher values on the other. From hermeticism this means employing both the higher mind and reason in their places, from McGilchrist a combination of focused study with the sense of higher values and appreciation of life. In terms of the *Corpus Hermeticum*, the higher mind responds at the level of the heart to the notion of the cosmos being formed out of love for beauty. The left hemisphere explores the text for details linking this cosmos to astrological symbolism in pursuit of a higher purpose. The notion of the divine world, the purely transcendent, being present in this world, immanent in rocks, plants, creatures, galaxies by way of *sympatheia*, is best appreciated by way of a sympathetic engagement with the hermetic sources and its adherents.

Chapter 2

Hermeticism: Historical Context and Key Themes

We thank you, supreme and most high god, by whose grace we
have attained the light of your knowledge...
Consciousness, by which we may know you;
Reason, by which we may seek you in our dim suppositions;
Knowledge, by which we may rejoice in knowing you.
Asclepius

This chapter sets out the main themes of hermeticism and briefly locates the source texts in their historical context. What were they and why were they so influential? At the heart of hermeticism is a creation story that describes the cosmos and the role of man in it. The cosmos is divine and single in essence, multiple in expression, and divine symbols are strewn throughout it. It is composed of three elements: matter, soul and spirit. The human soul is able to unite with spirit and matter by way of the dual composition of our mind. We and our cosmos are paradoxical in nature. Mankind can participate in the divine by way of the paradoxes in our own nature exemplified by mind and reason. We cultivate the mind or nous through reverence, whereas we understand the properties of the material world through reason. The cultivation of the reverent mind enables us to interpret the divine symbols through oracles, including the practice of astrology. The hermetic texts set out initiatic teachings whereby the acolyte is prepared to receive the divine word in his heart. Through preparation and initiation, the human soul sheds the negative attributes of the planets, taken on in the descent from the divine world at birth, and re-ascends a planetary, symbolic ladder back to our home in God. This view of the world provides a philosophical foundation for western astrology.

According to Nicholas Goodrick-Clarke,[1] hermeticism is a strand in western esotericism that tends to adopt key themes from the *Corpus Hermeticum* itself. This work was probably written in 3rd century AD Alexandria and presents sets of teachings that claim to originate with Hermes Trismegistus or the Thrice Greatest Hermes. Other hermetic sources include *The Asclepius, The Emerald Tablet* and the *Chaldean Oracles*. The documents that have survived to modern times are fragmentary and do not add up to a fully worked philosophy in any sense. The hermetic texts seem to offer a node or gathering point for ideas that are found in the works of Plato in 4th century BC and of the Neo-Platonists, amongst the Arab writers and mystics in the 8th to the 12th century AD and in the works of Marsilio Ficino in 15th century Florence. Subsequently they have continued to be very influential in a substratum of esoteric ideas up to the present day.[2]

The hermetic project is one of transmutation of lower, baser, and more material into higher, finer, and more spiritual. There are clear parallels with alchemy, which also flourished alongside hermeticism in Alexandria in late antiquity. Humanity is called to a regenerative work of re-ascension and reintegration with the divine ... Hermetic treatises present a guide or mentor figure who helps to raise souls by reawakening them to their divine nature, assisting in their spiritual transmutation, and leading them toward their heavenly destiny.[3]

The mentor or guide to the initiates is sometimes said to be Hermes Trismegistus, sometimes Poimandres. Peter Kingsley[4] sets out the etymology of the name Poimandres to show how it derives from the Egyptian gods Ra and Thoth and the Greek god Hermes. As Thoth, he was a moon god and governed the seasons and time, including the time of the flooding of the Nile, so essential for Egyptian agriculture. As ruler of time he also governed the lives of people and acted as psychopomp or guide of the souls of the dead to the world of the gods. He was also the origin of order, the lawgiver and judge. All magical and occult powers were part of his domain.[5] The Greek Hermes was also a psychopomp associated with the Moon. Both these deities were tricksters, inventive and playful, and this contributed to their popularity.

The hermetic creation story

This is the story of the creation of the cosmos, revealed to a narrator who is in an altered state of consciousness. "Thought came to me of the things that are and my thinking soared high and my bodily senses were restrained, like someone heavy with sleep from too much eating or toil of the body".[6] The revelation comes from no lesser being than Hermes Trismegistus, Poimandres himself. No wonder he soon says he was "terrified, out of my wits".[7]

First the cosmos is made in terms not dissimilar to the description in Genesis, with light and darkness, water, fire, smoke and earth and "from the light … a holy word mounted upon the <watery> nature".[8] At this point Poimandres says "In your mind you have seen the archetypal form, the preprinciple that exists before a beginning without end."[9] From this we move on to the generation of the solar system with the seven visible planets as governors.

> The mind who is god, being androgyne and existing as life and light, by speaking gave birth to a second mind, a craftsman, who, as god of fire and spirit, crafted seven governors; they encompass the sensible world in circles, and their government is called fate.[10]

The mind is a craftsman who whirls the planet governors in circles so that they then use the elements, particularly water and earth, to create the living things appropriate to air, earth and water. The scene is now set for the creation of Man. Man is like god[11] and therefore wishes to be a creator. In support of this

> the governors loved the man, and each gave a share of his
> own order. Learning well their essence and sharing in their
> nature, the man wished to break through the circumference
> of the circles ...[12]

The teaching continues with an exposition of the tripartite
nature of the cosmos and its paradoxical nature which man is
fitted to know by participating in the divine mind. It is with this
mind that God communicates through symbols, provided the
man has prepared himself as a fit receptacle.

> With this living thing alone does god converse, at night
> through dreams and through omens by day, and through
> all of them he foretells the future, through birds, through
> entrails, through inspiration, through the oak tree, whereby
> mankind also professes to know what has been, what is at
> hand and what will be.[13]

Man can be seduced by reason and the things of this world, for,
of these people we are told that

> their temperament is willful and angry, they feel no awe of
> things that deserve to be admired; they divert their attention
> to the pleasures and appetites of their bodies; and they
> believe that mankind came to be for such purposes.[14]

It is important that we choose mind in order to make ourselves
like God, since this mind can transport itself, via the imagination,
to all parts of the cosmos and even beyond it.

> So you must think of god in this way, as having everything
> – the cosmos, himself <the> universe – like thoughts within
> himself. Thus, unless you make yourself equal to god, you

cannot understand god; like is understood by like.[15]

God sows his seeds or symbols throughout the cosmos. "Clearly, the one who alone is unbegotten is also unimagined and invisible, but in presenting images of all things he is seen through all of them and in all of them".[16] This is the basis of the concept of *sympatheia*. It lies at the root of the possibility of sympathetic magic and the use of talismans. The things of this world participate in the divine by way of chains of sympathy whose action is that of daemonic spirits. Thus

> energies are like rays from god, natural forces like rays from the cosmos, arts and learning like rays from mankind … And this is the government of the universe, dependent from the nature of the one and spreading through the one mind.[17]

The human soul that descended from the divine realm as craftsman, carrying the nature of the planets, is intended ultimately to return and must surrender the negative planetary attributes along the way.

> Thence the human being rushes up through the cosmic framework, at the first zone surrendering the energy of increase and decrease [Moon]; at the second evil machination, [Mercury] a device now inactive; at the third the illusion of longing, [Venus] now inactive; at the fourth the ruler's arrogance, [Sun] now freed from excess; at the fifth unholy presumption and daring recklessness [Mars]; at the sixth the evil impulses that come from wealth, [Jupiter] now inactive; and at the seventh zone the deceit that lies in ambush [Saturn][18]

and declares "I have arrived, inspired with the divine breath of truth."[19]

In Part XIII of the *Corpus Hermeticum* the real preparation for oracle and divination is revealed as a second birth since "whoever through mercy has attained this godly birth and has forsaken bodily sensation recognizes himself as constituted of the intelligibles and rejoices".[20]

In this story the *Corpus Hermeticum* tells the hermetic myth, not in our modern sense of untrue but in Joseph Campbell's sense of a myth to live by.[21] It is a vision of life, of beauty, of struggle and of passion which allows the human a path of continuing development in adulthood and a creative role with God in the making of the world. The divine aspect is completely immaterial, yet it can exist in us just as thoughts, feelings and dreams can exist in us. The divine world is viewed as more important than the material because it is the source of the world and the source of all that we love and cherish in it since "For mankind … the ultimate standard is reverence, from which goodness follows."[22]

Symbol

We shall show them Our signs in the horizons and in themselves, till it is clear to them that it is the truth (*Quran*)

What is above is like what is below. What is below is like what is above. The miracle of unity is to be attained.
(*The Emerald Tablet,* Shah)

The nature of God is a circle of which the centre is everywhere, and the circumference nowhere. (Empedocles)

According to Scott[23] symbols are the mode in which God communicates with man. A symbolic awareness is therefore a part of the education of the true human. This is not to say that symbol can be expressed fully in terms other than the image itself. The apprehension of symbol is a speechless and enrapt moment, an awakening or enlightenment, an experience of the numinous that is at once my experience and at the same time not of me. It possesses rather than is possessed. Thus for Proclus, the inspired myths of Homer communicate their truth not by making images (eikones) and imitations (mimemata), but by making symbols (sumbola or sunthemata)[24] because symbols are not imitations of that which they symbolize'.[25]

In our world signs are usually intended to be unambiguous, such as traffic or exit signs. Symbols on the other hand are complex, purposeful and paradoxical. According to Uždavinys, "in the Chaldean Oracles, the sumbola are sown throughout the cosmos by the Paternal Demiurge and serve as the essential means of ascent and return to the gods;"[26] This is because "The Greek term sumbolon ... initially denoted a half of a whole object ... which could be joined with the other half in order that two contracting parties ... might have proof of their identity." [27]

In the context of the development of the true human

> one half ... represents the visible thing (the symbol proper) and the other half stands for the invisible noetic or supra-noetic reality symbolized by the lower visible part. The initiation and spiritual ascent consists in joining these two separate parts.[28]

This is possible because "Every soul was created by the Demiurge with harmonic ratios (*logoi*) and divine symbols (*sumbola theia*);[29] the *logoi* that constitute the soul's essence are *sumbola* and may be awakened through the theurgic rites".[30]

Symbols need to be appreciated in the context of the concept of *sympatheia*. In the Greek world this refers to:

> Certain chains or 'sympathies' between specific objects (symbols) and gods: These chains emanate from the gods (and so the idea of 'divine love' is often spoken of as causing or underlying *sympatheia*) ... Iamblichus considered the

community of the gods as an ineffable and supracosmic process which enabled sympathy to arise: 'one single bond of friendship, embracing the totality of being, effecting this bond through an ineffable process of communion'... In this holistic view of the cosmos, human friendship and 'sympathy for one's fellow human beings' are expressions and manifestations of divine love and providence; this, friendship, love and care for humanity are crucial for the theurgist.[31]

The whole world is permeated with these symbols that come under the governorship of the planetary daemons. Man is also filled with these properties on his descent from the divine realm. By journeying from heaven to earth and returning to the divine realm the soul reconciles the paradoxes of the universe, connecting time with eternity, being with becoming, matter with thoughts and knowledge that are immaterial. We might see the planetary symbols as the seven notes of the octave or the seven colours of the rainbow. Just as all music in the western world can be seen as depending upon the octave and all colours in nature and art as depending on the colours of the rainbow, so the planets are comprehensive in their governorship. All aspects of the world, material and immaterial, come under their sway. They articulate the raw material for the Demiurge's creative play.

We can harmonise ourselves with the divine totality, integrating the virtues of the planets into our nature and becoming a microcosm.

This teaching underlies the practice of genethliacal astrology as it was originally conceived. In the nativity, the 'Chaldeans' saw a chart of the astral bodies, as the journey through the planetary spheres had structured them. Correctly interpreted, this chart would reveal the native's constituent parts, material or subtle. It would speak of his daimon, the guardian angel who would accompany him on his voyage here below and watch over the fulfilment of his fate.[32]

In the hermetic creation story the earth has a real purpose. The earth is beautiful and loves the man as he is the realisation of her purpose.[33] The earth is also, in a sense, the revelation of the divine and infused with divinity in every part, yet this requires eyes to see and ears to hear. The human soul has to recognise the divine spirit in the world through symbols, and this calls for the cultivation of certain forms of attention.

Paradox, mind and reason

The hermetic cosmos is inherently paradoxical. This paradoxical universe can be known by man because we are ourselves paradoxical, having two modes of knowledge or perception. In the *Corpus Hermeticum* this is referred to as mind or nous and reason. Mind/nous/heart are what assimilate man to the divine realm, whereas discursive reason has a lesser and supporting function in this world. For example, "the many make philosophy obscure with the multiplicity of their reasoning",[34] whereas "the intelligible world, discernible only through mind's intuition, is incorporeal and … nothing corporeal can be combined with its nature."[35] What we are learning here concerns the knowledge of the divine ideas by way of the Intellect. Ideas are simply that: thoughts in a mind, intangible, but knowable by way of intuition.

The *Corpus Hermeticum* also says that those who honour both sides of their nature experience "discharge and release [from] the bonds of mortality so that god may restore us, pure and holy, to the nature of our higher part, to the divine."[36] This is because

> god shapes mankind from the nature of soul and of body, from the eternal and the mortal, in other words, so that the living being, so shaped can prove adequate to both its beginnings, wondering at heavenly beings and worshipping them, tending earthly beings and governing them.[37]

And then again, mankind is formed of both life and mortality and so is able "to tend to earth and to cherish divinity as well."[38] This is a view of the cosmos as earth-centred and therefore the earthly place of human consciousness. The divine may be seen here in the material world, through the craftwork of God the creator but God himself can only be known through something that He has implanted in man for the purpose, that which renders the human capable of self-realisation and fulfilment, of achieving his destiny.

Divination, initiation and astrology in the hermetic world

At the heart of the hermetic story is the initiatic conversation; now between Asclepius and Trismegistus, now with Poimandres and now with Tat. Much of this conversation concerns the nature of mind or nous, as compared with reason. Intellect is the function of this reverend mind, since "the intelligible world, discernible only through mind's intuition, is incorporeal".[39] Mind is a portal to a mystical vision of reality. The successful student Tat says to his father Hermes Trismegistus, "I no longer picture things with the sight of my eyes but with the mental energy that comes through the powers. I am in heaven, in earth, in water, in air; I am in animals and in plants; in the womb, before the womb, after the womb; everywhere."[40] There is a reciprocal relationship between this divine mind and the human mind, for in reality they are as one.

Iamblichus, writing in the 3rd century AD concerning his development of theurgy or god working as a combination of Greek and Egyptian spiritual practice, explains that the cultivation of the qualities of the theurgist are a lifelong work, entailing purification through ritual, intellectual and ethical means. The theurgist must be in a state of ritual receptivity, showing potential, sympathy and aptitude. This is necessary for working with symbols. "The central premise of theurgy is that an affinity (ultimately deriving from divine love) between the symbol and its respective deity allows the attraction of divine power into the practitioner's soul."[41] Oracles and inspired divination were fundamental aspects of the philosophy of the Neo-Platonists.

> Rationality and revelation were considered to be interlinked and complementary, mutually inclusive ... for Porphyry and Iamblichus, oracles constituted symbols ... of the gods, which comprised tools for philosophical contemplation, insight and initiation. [From this perspective divination is an] essential element of mystical union with the divine.[42]

We are here dealing with a higher order of wisdom and truthfulness. "Platonic conceptions of divinity often involved an intrinsic association of divinity with truth" as "Apollo, god of oracles and truth *par excellence* could not lie."[43]

Astrology has a special role within this scheme, since it is the means whereby "the gods issue cultic instructions to mortals regarding their correct worship".[44] Ritual instructions are based on an astrological determination of the correct timing of the event. This is only possible through the concept of sympathy discussed above and also by way of the quality, preparation and receptivity of the practitioner. Actions carried out with proper preparation and initiation distinguish the true theurgist from the magician.[45] The theurgist is under divine guidance and providence; the magician seeks power in the material world alone. In the hermetic context, we can see that this is a distinction that makes all the difference between valid ritual and sacrilege. This essential distinction will later be picked up by Marsilio Ficino in his *Disputation against the Judgements of Astrologers*. The quality of judgement depends on the quality of the astrologer, and it is this point that makes the discrimination of who is, or is not, a hermetic astrologer ambiguous or even unknowable. In this context there was a close and mutually respectful relationship between philosophers and astrologers.

Crystal Addey told us that:

Divination and philosophy were deeply connected in the Ancient World. Philosophy was used for the interpretation of Oracles: the intellectual thought and personal reflection of the enquirer was a vital part of the experience of consulting an oracle. Philosophers argued for the truth and usefulness of oracles, astrology and other forms of divination. Philosophers were sometimes Priests at Oracle sanctuaries and often used divination in ritual practices. Philosophers wrote/compiled Collections of Oracles as a philosophical tool for reflection and divine wisdom. Philosophers themselves consulted oracles.[46]

One of the most striking passages in the *Corpus Hermeticum* concerns the fate of the world if we fail to cultivate the mind and reverence the Gods, for then the Gods will turn their backs on us and walk away.

> How mournful when the gods withdraw from mankind! Only the baleful angels remain … to mingle with humans, seizing the wretches and driving them to every outrageous crime – war, looting, trickery and all that is contrary to the nature of souls. Then neither will the earth stand firm nor the sea be sailable; stars will not cross heaven nor will the course of the stars stand firm in heaven. Every divine voice will grow mute in enforced silence. The fruits of the earth will rot; the soil will no more be fertile; and the very air will droop in gloomy lethargy.[47]

Some commentators consider that this powerful text is best understood in the context of its time and place of origin, when the Egyptian religion and culture seemed under threat of destruction from the Roman occupation and the Christian desire for conformity of belief. However, I suggest that it has an abiding power to speak to our own time, which suffers from the loss of reverence and the creative power of nous and is faced with the overwhelming fears generated by man-made damage to the living systems of the earth.

Chapter 3

Marsilio Ficino and his Hermetic Astrological Practice

Marsilio Ficino was born near Florence in 1433. His father was physician to Cosimo de' Medici, one of the richest and most influential men in Europe at the time. Ficino was fascinated with the philosophy and writings of Plato and particularly excited by the platonic knowledge brought to Europe by Gemistus Plethon, the envoy of the Byzantine Empire. Cosimo was inspired by Plethon with the idea of refounding the Platonic Academy in Florence. He sent out scouts to Byzantium to buy and return with books written by Plato and his followers. Above all he was keen to track down hermetic texts, since in Europe, at that time, only the Asclepius was available. Cosimo appointed the young Ficino to be his translator, a task that Ficino readily undertook, fostering the revived Academy at the Villa Carreggi outside Florence, as a way of reanimating the spiritual life of his time with Platonic and hermetic ideas.[1]

Marsilio Ficino was a Dominican priest and did not lay claim to being an astrologer. Indeed, he wrote, but never published, a condemnation of astrologers in the *Disputation against the Judgements of Astrologers*.[2] Nevertheless, his writing, particularly his many letters, are full of astrological references and exhortations to use astrological symbolism. In this he was treading a dangerous line. Thomas Aquinas had condemned the practice of astrology in the Christian world in the 13th century, drawing on earlier classical writers who interpreted Aristotle as describing a causal cosmos, removing God as the source of planetary rays. For Ficino, astrologers following this tradition, based on Ptolemy's *Tetrabiblos*, practised a 'literalisation' of astrology and thereby "subsumed an essentially divinatory core of symbolic meaning into a dominant Aristotelian model of natural scientific 'cause and effect'."[3] Brockbank cites O. Pederson saying "In the *Tetrabiblos* 'the principles of astrology were described in a secular manner without mythological or religious overtones'."[4] This view of the cosmos was taken up

> by a Stoical determinist tradition of astrology, where ... the cosmos, stripped of its gods, became a natural scientific rather than divine structure ... known through human reason ... interpretations were given material bases [and caused] human action in the same way as they caused natural phenomena such as tides or weather.[5]

This natural way of knowing the world was tolerated by the Christian church, but any hint of a "superhuman foresight or 'unnatural' kind of knowing, could only be a sin as it usurped the prerogative of God."[6]

Ficino knew the official line and in his writings he constantly qualifies his astrological advice by saying this is purely a work of nature, or he hides his own opinions behind those of his classical sources, saying he not so much says these things as reports the opinions of others. In his *Three Books on Life* he thinks it prudent to remind the reader that "In all things which I discuss here or elsewhere, I intend to assert only so much as is approved by the Church."[7]

In the golden thread of hermeticism Ficino found "Nothing less than a combination of 'learning and keenness of mind' and 'sanctity of life and reverence for the divine'; in other words, a combination of intellectual penetration and religious devotion."[8] It is this combination of these two distinct attitudes towards the world that are the mark of his hermetic interpretation. On the one hand his "astrological framework is specific and his instructions technical – not only must one study the nature of the planets, but be able to calculate their movements and observe their configurations."[9] but this must be accompanied by an act of spiritual will and desire, so that the stellar pattern becomes a living symbol.[10]

Ficino, as an expert classicist, knew that, for his ancient sources, astrology was informed by the concept of *sympatheia*, a term he sometimes expresses as quintessence or as baits.[11] The cosmos for him is, as Plato describes it, "an animal more unified than any other animal, the most perfect animal".[12] He feels a calling to revive the life of the church and his world, by way of a reanimation of the spirit in the world, which he links with daemonic powers.

> For Ficino, Platonic philosophy was a vital intellectual preparation for the ultimate revelation of the Christian faith, and he believed he had been sent by Divine Providence to revitalise religion through its revival.[13]

With reference to daemonic spirits he tells us

> a natural cause does not channel the confluence of these mutually diverse factors to one end, but rather a daemonic cause; ... the cause assists the heavens by always providing the means to effect the end already known to the heavenly understanding, and also its own power to effect the end, which the motion of the heavens often does not make happen, but merely signifies.[14]

Ficino seeks to show that

> astrology is not causal or mechanistic at all, but metaphoric and divinatory. If the stars indicate divine will in the manner

of omens and oracles, revealing the path of good fortune to those who can engage imaginatively with their patterns, then astrology enters the domain of the sacred.[15]

Ficino's 'internalisation' of the heavens

arose through his assimilation of the Hermetic teachings concerning the soul's dynamic – and initiatory – relationship to the cosmos in its descent to embodiment and ascent to God through the seven spheres … the perennial wisdom which was believed to have been transmitted from Zoroaster and Hermes Trismegistus through Pythagoras and Orpheus, reaching 'absolute perfection' in the teachings of Plato – was revered precisely because it gave voice to a vital, personal connection between humans and the divine realm through the analogous correspondence of macrocosm and microcosm.[16]

For Ficino then

the whole of astrology is nothing other than the translation of reality into celestial language, an illustrated projection of the whole, in which the fantastic figures of the imagination transcribe the movements of the psyche, the stirring of the affection, the processes of the generation, the chains of concepts …[17]

The fantastic figures of the imagination are immaterial and in that sense closer to the divine world. We are probably better to think of them as 'imaginal' in the sense used by Henri Corbin, as distinct from fantasy.[18]

To appreciate Ficino as an exemplar of hermetic astrology is therefore not to translate his practice simply as a form of astrological technique, for Ficino practised many techniques. It is rather an approach, based on philosophical premises and in particular on the idea of chains of sympathy, operated by daemonic intelligences derived from the One God. Ficino would be the first to condemn the idea of a materialistic astrology in which the planets, in their physicality, are causes of actions in this world, leading men to be fated from birth. Rather he urges us that with

> a little additional preparation ... to capture the gifts of the celestials, [or planetary daemons] provided each accommodates himself to that gift in particular to which he is particularly subject.[19]

The gift to which we are subject is found from the ruling planet of our birth chart. Ficino applied hermetic axioms of sympathy, the tripartite cosmos and the paradoxical nature of mind, to the idea of the planets as signs rather than causes. He uses his cosmological understanding to identify the soul qualities of a person and enable them to align their lives with the heavens; protecting them from difficult planetary transits; electing the auspicious moment for any action, making music, talismans, and performing theurgic ritual with planetary symbols for initiatic purposes.

Ficino's cosmos and the mind

In Book 3, Chapter I of *Three Books on Life,* Ficino describes the tripartite nature of the cosmos as composed of Body, Soul and Intellect. He explains for us here that the nature of "Intellect is absolutely motionless, ... and very far away from the Body"[20] and "Body is in itself powerless ... and far removed from Intellect". It is only the Soul that unites them. Soul is the "Primum Mobile and movable of herself, of her own accord." Soul is also "the mean of things, in her own fashion she contains all things and is proportionally ... near to both. Therefore, she is equally connected with everything, even with those things which are at a distance from one other, because they are not at a distance from her."[21] On account of this permeation of the divine and material worlds, the soul possesses knowledge of "Ideas in the Divine Mind". Ficino explains that "if at any time the species degenerates from its proper form, it can be formed again ... through the Idea as intermediary".[22] In this way he offers us the possibility of healing, since our original Idea comes from God and cannot be anything other than perfect. Likewise he goes on to tell us that

> if in the proper manner you bring to bear on a species ... many things which are dispersed but which conform to the same Idea ... you will soon draw a particular gift from the Idea, through the seminal reason of the Soul.[23]

In this way he indicates to us the realm of sympathies, spreading throughout the world on account of the activity of the soul. Through this we can make talismans, eat foods, make music or perform actions that awaken the divine Idea in us, restoring us to wholeness.

Ficino, in his commentary on Plato's *Symposium*, talks about the double light of the soul, saying:

> Once the soul has been created by God, she turns towards Him as her Father through a natural prompting, just as fire, produced on Earth through the power of higher things, immediately directs itself towards the higher realms under a natural impulse. When the soul has turned to God, she is illumined by His rays; but when this initial splendour is accepted into the substance of the soul ... the soul sees herself and all that is beneath her, ... yet she cannot see what is above her.
>
> But having been brought closer to God by means of this first spark, the soul receives a second and brighter light, by which she may come to know what is above. Thus she

has two lights, natural and supernatural. When these are conjoined, the soul may soar on them, as if they were two wings, through the heavenly realm.[24]

For mankind the knowledge of the soul is not automatic. Ficino takes up the hermetic story in one of his letters saying that "Mercurius Trismegistus, the wisest of all the Egyptians" and Plato consider that souls were originally in the divine realm "steadfastly contemplating the eternal mind of God"[25] where they were "well nourished with perfect knowledge ... fed on ambrosia and nectar". However,

> souls are depressed into bodies through thinking about and desiring earthly things. [They] drink continuously of the river Lethe, that is forgetfulness of the divine. They do not fly back to heaven ... until they begin to contemplate once more those divine natures which they have forgotten.[26]

This requires "moral conduct and ... contemplation". These are the two wings of the philosopher's mind which Ficino traces back to Socrates. On recovery of these wings, the soul is drawn away from earth by 'divine frenzy'.[27] To Plato he attributes the idea that "men never remember the divine unless they are stirred by its shadows or images, as they may be described, which are perceived by the bodily senses."[28] Ficino explores these ideas in some detail, explaining that we remember our true spiritual origin by way of the things we see in the world. However, we ought not to admire material things in themselves, for these are no more than shadows of the divine reality, and

> Plato holds it the mark of a dull mind and corrupt state if a man desires no more than the shadows of that beauty nor looks for anything beyond the form his eyes can see.[29]

For Ficino, as well as two wings, the mind has two modes of

operation derived from his hermetic sources. These are variously characterised as "'learning and keenness of mind' and 'sanctity of life and reverence for the divine'; in other words, a combination of intellectual penetration and religious devotion."[30]

Divine paradox

Ficino expresses his sense of the paradoxical nature of divinity in a letter to Michele Mercati.[31] In this letter he describes his own struggles with faith in his earlier life in the form of a dialogue of his soul with God. Is he perhaps, in this sense, aligning himself with the start of the *Corpus Hermeticum* where the author dialogues with pure mind in the form of Poimandres? He follows the hermetic idea in illustrating the paradoxical nature of divinity with expressions such as

> Your father is the least of all things in size, just as he is the greatest of all things in excellence; and since he is very small he is within everything, but since his is very great he is outside everything ... I fill and am not filled, for I am fullness itself. I penetrate and am not penetrated, for I am the power of penetration itself. I contain and am not contained, for I am containing itself ... I am also able to enter and permeate ... being unity itself, through which all things are made and endure, and which all things seek.[32]

Ficino's deity goes on to say that the soul must not be content with any partial knowledge of God. It must "resist the body", not content itself with the mind or intellect for "you ascend by understanding and love beyond any kind of intellect, to life itself, pure existence, absolute being." It is a conceptual notion of the divine as the good, which is manifested throughout the material world. Ficino tells Mercati "do you desire to look on the face of good? Then look around at the whole universe, full of the light of the sun"[33] and from here all materiality of vision must be gradually removed in imagination until the soul attains to pure light which "confers life on all, seeing that its very shadow is the light of this sun." The sun therefore leads us in imagination towards its source. "It loves each single thing, for each single thing is especially its own."[34]

The Sun

One of the last books Ficino wrote was the *Book of the Sun,* but he had very definite ideas about the Sun in his earlier works as well. He follows the *Corpus Hermeticum* again here. For instance, he explains:

> our own soul ... puts forth a general force of life everywhere within us – especially through the heart as the source of fire which is the nearest thing to the soul. In the same way the World-soul, which is active everywhere, unfolds in every place its power of universal life principally through the Sun. Accordingly ... the entire Soul, both in us and in the universe, dwells in any member but most of all in the heart and in the Sun."[35]

In the *Corpus Hermeticum* we find "Eternity, therefore, is an image of god; the cosmos is an image of eternity; and the sun is an image of the cosmos. The human is an image of the sun."[36] This sense of the centrality of the Sun, which for Ficino is a physical reality as well as a philosophical one, leads him to propose remedies that are particularly solar. He tells us that the human species is primarily solar, citing the Arab astrologers, and goes on to substantiate this idea saying man is "erect and beautiful, from his subtle humors and the clearness of his sprit, from the perspicuity of his imagination and his pursuit of truth and honor."[37] In order to make ourselves more solar then we can "drink in unconditionally the power of the Sun and to some extent the natural power of the Solar daemons."[38] We do this by associating ourselves with solar things and he lists lions or cocks, Phoebean plants, "metals and gems and vapor and hot air", citing Proclus as his authority. He refers to the "chain of beings [that] descends by levels from any star, of the firmament through any planet under its dominion."[39] Note that his chain is of beings or daemons, not of things, and it is this that makes his cosmology hermetic and spiritual rather than purely physical.

Ficino is well aware of natal astrology as well as the movements of the planets. For instance, he tells us that "Solar are those people … who are born when Leo is ascending and the Sun either is in it or aspects it".[40] He is also familiar with the solar return and with ingress charts, for he tells us that "as soon as the Sun enters the same minute, [as the birth time] they [the astrologers] think that the man is, as it were, reborn; and thence they prophesy his year's fortune."[41] In a similar way he suggests that we can think of the world being reborn "when the Sun has reached the first minute of Aries."[42] This tells us that his astrology is both material, having regard to the positions of the planets, and divinatory, yielding symbolic meanings.

Triumph over Fate

"All things are directed from goodness to goodness. Rejoice in the present; set no value on property, seek no honours. Avoid excess; avoid activity. Rejoice in the present."
Maxim on the walls of the Villa Careggi[43]

One of the most potent astrological ideas that Ficino offered the people of his time was the idea that they could work with the properties in their birth chart to turn aside the worst effects of their astrological fate. In a letter he says "someone may say it is foolish to wish to contend against unassailable fate. I, however, reply that it can be opposed as easily as one may wish to oppose it."[44]

He goes on to compare the movement of the spheres with the possibility that he who puts them under examination seems already to have transcended them, to have come near to God Himself ... guided, now by the providence of God that is above the heavens, and now by the freedom of the mind.[45]

Ficino was motivated to apply this maxim to himself by the onerous nature of his own birth chart as understood in traditional terms. For instance, he writes to Giovanni Cavalcanti that

Saturn seems to have impressed the seal of melancholy on me from the beginning; set, as it is, almost in the midst of

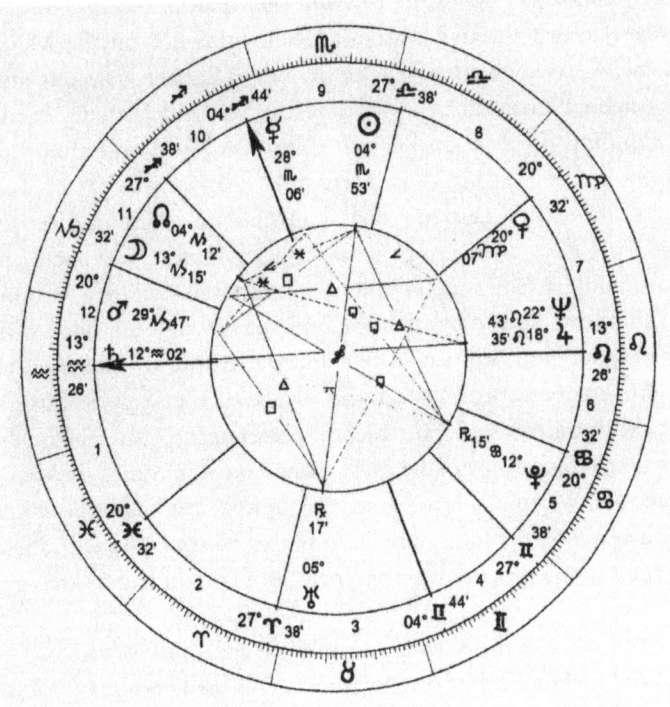

The birth chart of Marcilio Ficino as displayed in *Marcilio Ficino*, edited and introduced by Angela Voss (North Atlantic Books, 2006)

my ascendant Aquarius, it is influenced by Mars, also in Aquarius, and the Moon in Capricorn. It is in square aspect to the Sun and Mercury in Scorpio, which occupy the ninth house.[46]

From an astrological point of view, Saturn would be associated with limits and with fears. In his ascendant it affects his body, his health and his personality. Saturn is at home in Aquarius, meaning its powers are strong; in other words it can be very limiting and make the native, the person whose chart this is, very fearful. Mars and Saturn are considered malefic or infortunes, so they tend to bring out the worst in the situation: Mars through anger, Saturn through restraint. Their influence on the Moon is likely to adversely affect his mood. A square aspect is also considered stressful, so a square to the Sun and Mercury exerts a grinding pressure on his self-expression (Sun) and ability to think and express his ideas (Mercury).[47]

Ficino would certainly have known about these qualities in his chart from an early age.[48] His father Diotifeci, was doctor to Cosimo de' Medici and would have integrated astrology with his medical understanding. It is the sense of having been born with this astrological stigmatism that motivated him to find ways to legitimately escape or modify his own fate. One way to do this was to counterpose a more helpful planet against the malefic. In his *Three Books on Life* he says "when you fear Mars, set Venus opposite. When you fear Saturn, use Jupiter."[49] When he says this, he is applying the full symbolic array that he associates with these planets in the process. He even includes a kind of dance, saying

and see to it that you engage in some continual motion … and make sure that your own motion is the opposite of the external motions which are secretly going to harm you, and that you imitate so far as possible the action of the heavens.[50]

Ficino closes a letter to Giovanni Cavalcanti saying

> I see that you are again … urging me to sing another hymn
> of recantation to Saturn … I shall say … that a nature of this
> kind does not issue from Saturn; or … I shall … say that this
> nature itself is a unique and divine gift.[51]

It could be a gift for Ficino in the sense that Saturn, as the furthest
sphere from the earth, is also closest to the divine realm, close
to what Corbin refers to as the eighth clime[52] or the sphere of
the fixed stars[53] and He therefore favours divine contemplation.

Music was a vital part of Ficino's practical and spiritual
project. In a letter to Antonio Canigiani,[54] he links music to its
origin in Apollo, god of the Sun, who is also the "discoverer of
medicine" saying "Apollo, by his vital rays, bestows health and
life on all and drives away disease" and he goes on to say that by
sounding the strings of the lyre, Apollo regulates the seasons. He
goes into great detail about the connections between music, body
and soul since

> music takes place in reason, the second in fantasy, and the third
> in words; thence follows song and after that the movement of
> the fingers in sound. Lastly the movement of the whole body
> in gymnastics or dancing. Thus, we may see that the music of
> the soul is led by steps to all the limbs of the body.

Lest we should imagine Ficino in wild dancing frenzy, he tells
Canigiani that

> Plato does, however, criticize plaintive and light music on
> the grounds that it leads to lack of spirit, lechery, and bad
> temper. But he recommends solemn and calming music as
> the most wholesome medicine for spirit, soul and body.

For this reason, Ficino will

> often resort to the solemn sound of the lyre and to singing,

to avoid other sensual pleasures entirely … to raise the mind to the highest considerations and to God as much as I may.

Allen tells us that Ficino's Orphic hymns were to be accompanied by fumigations which have

a long and complex history in cult practices all over the world, and a number of the fumigants enjoined in the hymns are rich in medical, magical and religious associations.[55]

Claiming to follow Plotinus, Ficino would offer "frankincense and manna to the Sun, styrax to Saturn and to Jupiter, myrrh to Neptune, and frankincense again to Mercury". Allen suggests that Ficino did not publish these instructions precisely because they might be thought of as

rendering visible daemonic forms which might grace the worshipper with their presence, if the daemons were so inclined and the aromas were to their particular liking … Ficino was demonstrably familiar with vapors, hazes, sprays, sacred dusts, and powders of various kinds, all of which could function in essentially the same way.[56]

In this place Ficino is not simply aspiring to assimilate himself to heaven but hoping to invite heavenly intelligences to earth. This is a practice he could have obtained authority for from the *Asclepius* where Hermes Trismegistus tells Asclepius how humans make idols

from a mixture of plants, stones and spices … that have in them a natural power of divinity … those gods are entertained with constant sacrifices, with hymns, praises and sweet sounds in tune with heaven's harmony: so that the heavenly ingredient enticed into the idol by constant communication with heaven may gladly endure its long stay among human kind.[57]

The point of this activity is so that

> our gods render aid to humans as if through loving kinship,
> looking after some things individually, foretelling some
> things through lots and divination, and planning ahead to
> give help by other means, each in his own way.[58]

All in all, Ficino applies the concept of *sympatheia* throughout
his cosmological and astrological understanding. He invites the
immaterial and divine daemons of the planets to his aid, with a
symbolic practice. The quality of the emotion we invest in our
talismans, songs and vapours is a key ingredient. He refers to

> the intention of the imagination [saying] if anyone ... yearns
> vehemently to get help from it and believes with all his heart
> and hopes with all his strength, he will surely get a great deal
> more help from it ... The human spirit is transformed into
> this Jovial spirit by an affect which is love ... [therefore] the
> love and faith of the sick person towards the doctor ... are
> very conducive to health.[59]

In this sense he is almost proposing something like the placebo
effect which has been found to be a contributory factor in modern
healing.[60] In a postscript on *Freedom from Care,* Ficino urges his
readers on what we might interpret today as stress management:

> live joyfully in the present, day by day. For worry about
> present circumstances both snatches the present from you
> and takes away your future ... Heaven's joy has created you
> ... By your joy heaven will preserve you.[61]

In this Chapter I have indicated ways in which Ficino's
appreciation of the golden thread of hermeticism illuminated his
astrological understanding and practices. In the next I will explore
the resonances of hermeticism and astrology in the present day.

Chapter 4

Hermeticism, Astrology and Modern Man

God is dead ... and we have killed him ... How shall we,
murderers of all murderers, console ourselves? ... Who will wipe
this blood off us? With what water could we purify ourselves? What
festival of atonement, what sacred games shall we need to invent?
Friedrich Nietzsche: *Parable of the Madman*

At this point it is necessary to pull the threads together
and look at whether there can be a hermetic astrology for
our time. The question is challenging if not impossible in
that, as Geoffrey Cornelius has set out in *Field of Omens*,[1]
there is no presentiment, no cultural readiness in our major
institutions, to accept that astrology might have any validity
at all, either in theory or in practice. How then can there be
one for our time?

Other elements of the hermetic perspective have equally
been devalued and slipped from public discourse. Matter is what
matters now, whereas soul and spirit are intangible and therefore
not of overriding importance in our collective decision making.[2]
The re-establishment of the presentiment of a hermetic astrology
depends on the re-establishment of the philosophical perspective
in which it once found its place.

This chapter sets out some ways in which elements of
this perspective are affirmed in our time by the work of Iain
McGilchrist[3] on neuroscience, and the work of C.G. Jung[4] on
psychoanalysis. An inclusive, paradoxical, both/and perspective

is a vital aspect of hermetic mysticism. Iain McGilchrist sets out how both/and perspectives are hard-wired into our brains and shows, with the help of Max Scheler's pyramid of values,[5] the way our two modes of thinking associate with matter, values and ultimately the Holy. He also makes it abundantly clear he considers our prevailing cultural perspective to be dangerously one-sided in favour of rationalist, left-brain thinking.

The work of Jung is equally important in reasserting the mediating role of the psyche or soul and the importance of dreams as a place where symbols have the capacity to expose us to the numinous, to qualities of experience that are compelling, perplexing and impervious to reason. They take us into the right hemisphere world. Astrology is at all times symbolic work demanding both right and left hemisphere modes of thinking, allowing us to conjure with complexity in ourselves and in our world.

If the presentiment of astrology depends upon our ability to work with paradox, with both/add thinking, then this is taken into the heart of government decision making in the work of Professor Jake Chapman.[6] He encourages public policy makers to take account of the complex and adaptive behaviours of living systems, coded for only in the right hemisphere of the brain. He challenges the idea that human systems can be designed in the same way as a mechanism, the left-brain approach.

A hermetic astrology has to take account of the paradoxical and employ both/and thinking. It is adaptive and therefore liberating from a mechanistic and fated perspective. To do this, astrology must be a work with symbols rather than signs. Astrology then becomes a work that offers a developmental, psychological and spiritual dimension for both practitioner and clients, aspiring to an assimilation to the cosmos as sacred, by way of *sympatheia* and the divination of the path of good fortune.

The mind and McGilchrist

In his book *The Master and His Emissary,*[7] Iain McGilchrist takes the metaphor of master and emissary to explore the role of the two hemispheres of our brain. He shows how they bring into reality two distinct world views. Although the two hemispheres overlap in function on nearly every issue, they do so in different ways and with different outcomes. By adopting one or other mode of attention to the world, we actually generate very different worlds for ourselves and, in a sense, shift between two different subpersonalities. In addition, McGilchrist shows us that the narrow-minded and controlling emissary, the left hemisphere, can dominate and negate the wise master, the right hemisphere. The consequence of this is ultimately catastrophic, not least because the left hemisphere is unable to take on board or generate any new thinking and is therefore powerless to solve the problems it witnesses or creates.

To understand how this is so and bring out some of the parallels with mind and reason in the *Corpus Hermeticum* we need to set out the characteristics of both hemispheres very briefly. The left hemisphere we might compare with reason in the hermetic texts. Its focus is on the material world and particularly with making use of the world and manipulating it for our benefit.[8] In order to do this we need to be selective about what we see, in order to focus in on the useful elements. The left hemisphere is therefore biased toward identification by parts rather than wholes.[9] It takes things literally and prefers to classify things in broad categories such as useful/useless. It tends towards abstraction in the sense of taking things out of their context. The left hemisphere has a tendency to make divisions in knowledge where there are none in nature. On this basis it "draws mistaken conclusions from the information available to it and lays down the law about what only the right hemisphere can know."[10] It does this because it needs to be right, yet this sense of rightness and certainty is related to narrowness of view.[11] Notice the phrase 'needs to be right', indicating that there is a sense of a distinct personality at work here. McGilchrist is saying that the ego personality, at this moment is identified with this 'need'. "The left hemisphere likes things that are man-made. Things we make are also more certain: we know them inside out, because we put them together."[12] They are not, like living things, constantly changing and moving beyond our grasp.

> [The] left hemisphere is unconcerned about others and their
> feelings: 'social intercourse is conducted with a blanket disregard
> for the feelings, wishes, needs and expectations of others'.[13]

The only emotion associated with the left hemisphere is anger. We can compare these traits with the description in the *Corpus Hermeticum* of the people of reason alone:

> their temperament is willful and angry, they feel no awe of
> things that deserve to be admired; they divert their attention
> to the pleasures and appetites of their bodies; and believe
> that mankind came to be for such purposes.[14]

We might compare what McGilchrist says about the right hemisphere with the attributes of mind or nous in the *Corpus Hermeticum*. The right hemisphere makes sense of things in the round and in context. It is attuned to things as they are in the world in their uniqueness, dealing with individuals as gestalt wholes. [15] It is able to take in new information, which it does, non-judgementally.[16] The right hemisphere is therefore the learning hemisphere, engaged in processing new information and is able to explore "an array of possible solutions [to a problem], which remain live while alternatives are explored".[17]

The right hemisphere brings together different elements, including information from the ears, eyes, and other sensory organs, and from memory, so as to generate the richly complex, but coherent, world we experience. It has a broader field of attention, open to whatever may be, and this, coupled with greater integration over time and space, is what makes possible the recognition of broad or complex patterns, the perception of the 'thing as a whole', seeing the wood for the trees.[18]

It perceives the emotional significance of events and is able to connect with complex and ambiguous symbols.[19] It is better able to accommodate the paradoxical nature of the world, for example via concepts of time and eternity. McGilchrist writes:

> Music takes place in time. Yet music also has the capacity to make us stand outside time ... Perhaps this going 'through' a thing to find its opposite is an aspect of the right hemisphere world, in which 'opposites' are not incompatible, an aspect of its roundness rather than linearity ... time itself is ... paradoxical in nature, and ... music does not so much free time from temporality as bring out an aspect that is always present within time, its intersection with a moment which partakes of eternity ... [It brings] out the spirituality latent in what we conceive as physical existence, and uncover[s] the universality that is, as Goethe spent a lifetime trying to express, always latent in the particular ... music ... is used to communicate with the supernatural, with whatever is by definition above, beyond, 'Other than', ourselves.[20]

McGilchrist tells us that the left hemisphere deals with explicit meanings only, whereas the right hemisphere deals with the implicit and metaphor.

> The importance of metaphor is that it *underlies all forms of understanding whatsoever*, science and philosophy no less than poetry and art ... The realm of all that remains, and has to remain, implicit and ambiguous is extensive, and is crucially important. This is why one feels so hopeless

relying on the written word to convey meaning in humanly important and emotionally freighted situations.[21]

McGilchrist cites the pyramid of values developed by the philosopher Max Scheler and maps the worlds engendered by the hemispheres onto it. "The priorities of the left hemisphere map exclusively onto the lowest level of this pyramid. Here we have the values concerning whether something is pleasant and whether it is useful."[22] McGilchrist associates the right hemisphere with all the higher values in this pyramid and with the ability to deal with paradox. The right hemisphere responds to a range of emotions related to bonding and empathy so, "in the absence of a functioning right hemisphere, our world and ourselves become emotionally impoverished."[23]

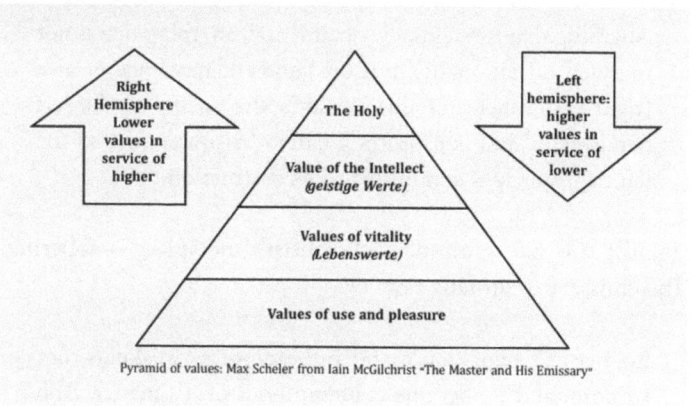

Pyramid of values: Max Scheler from Iain McGilchrist "The Master and His Emissary"

Moral values are preferentially the priority of the right hemisphere "linked to the capacity for empathy, ... deeply bound up with our emotional sensitivity to others. Empathy is intrinsic to morality."[24]

In terms of the two modes of knowing and values, Jeremy Naydler writes that

we live today at a time of increasing polarisation between,

on the one hand, the reductionist philosophy of scientific materialism, so prevalent in the media and so dominant in our academic institutions, and on the other hand philosophies, many of which draw on very ancient traditions, that acknowledge the reality of inner worlds.[25]

Being preoccupied with "inner worlds" is not a mainstream activity in our time and yet Naydler sees it as of vital importance to us, not simply in terms of 'ultimate meanings' but also

our orientation towards the kind of food we eat, how we want our children to be educated, the kind of medicines we take, the buildings we design and a host of other extremely practical and down to earth things.[26]

Anything that is essentially sacramental, anything that is not founded on rationality, but on bonds of reverence or awe (right-hemisphere terrain) becomes the enemy of the left hemisphere, and constitutes a bar to its supremacy; so the left hemisphere is committed to its destruction.[27]

Against this background, McGilchrist's metaphor is sobering. The emissary eventually saw

his master's temperance and forbearance as weakness, not wisdom, and ... became contemptuous of his master. And so it came about that the master was usurped, the people were duped, the domain became a tyranny; and eventually it collapsed in ruins.[28]

McGilchrist states that the left brain cannot generate anything new and is therefore fated to constantly recycle old ideas. He would identify symbolic awareness and spiritual purpose as the domain of the right brain hemisphere. This hemisphere is also the only route to new thinking and therefore vital for addressing the problems of our age in new and creative ways. Professor Jake Chapman compares the results of two modes of thinking, tied to two sets of metaphor, in public services in the UK.

The way to visualise the difference between the mechanistic, linear approach to policy and the holistic, systemic approach is to compare the results of throwing a rock and a live bird. Mechanical linear models are excellent for understanding where the rock will end up, but useless for predicting the trajectory of a bird – even though both are subject to the same laws of physics. To the degree that social and organisational systems, like the NHS, show adaptive behaviours they are better regarded as similar to live birds than lumps of rock.[29]

He uses the machine metaphor to describe problematic and inappropriate ways of addressing problems. From McGilchrist we can see that this is a preferred left hemisphere approach. On the other hand, adaptive behaviours are the domain of the right hemisphere. Chapman's metaphor of the living bird is helpful to us when thinking about Ficino's hermetic and theurgic approach to astrological practice. On the one hand the bird feels the throw and initially moves in that direction, not unlike Ficino's understanding of the initial effect of Saturn in his birth chart. However, Ficino makes an adaptive response to the situation, based on his understanding of the best possibilities available to him practically and symbolically. This makes the outcome harder to predict but likely to be more auspicious for him.

Chapman in his teaching on complexity and soft systems practice in the public service observes that:

> People find it hard to face the uncertainty, ambiguity and different views of what is happening in complex situations … The most common ways of avoiding complexity are to presume simple causation of the issue (when in fact there are multiple interacting causes), to adopt an ideological position or to make use of stereotypes that evoke prejudices used in justifying a simplistic "solution". However it is achieved,

the consequences are, that a policy or intervention that ignores complexity will generate a plethora of *unintended consequences*. These arise because the simple causation or solutions presumed by the advocate do not match the reality of what is occurring in the real world.[30]

This is clearly a consequence of unbridled left hemisphere thinking. Again, there is a parallel with Ficino's *Disputation against the Judgements of Astrologers*, where he argues for the complexity and difficulty in judging from the stars, saying "the stars are innumerable and all act … But we have only – and imperfectly – observed seven planets in addition to the stars in the constellations."[31]

There are many ways in which McGilchrist sees the Renaissance as

a huge expansion of the right hemisphere's way of being in the world, into which, initially, the work of the left hemisphere is integrated. And it is this that accounts for the astonishing fertility and richness, as well as the remarkable breadth of concern, to this day memorialized in the concept of the Renaissance man.[32]

Ficino's translations and interpretations of the Platonic and hermetic texts played a crucial role in this development.

Jung and astrology

Vocatus atque non vocatus, Deus aderit
Called or uncalled, God will be present
Carved by Jung above the door of his house in Kusnacht,
Switzerland[33]

C.G. Jung is a seminal figure in the development of psychoanalysis in the twentieth century, and much has been written about his interest in astrology, divination and the western esoteric tradition. I will therefore simply give brief indications as to the ways in which his thought parallels the nature of the hermetic cosmos or gives value to the practice of a hermetic astrology.

Leon Schlamm describes Jung as "a secular (post-religious) Western visionary mystic".[34] In this role he addresses, in new and creative ways, the "disenchantment of the world" by "rationalisation and intellectualisation".[35] Jung himself laments this situation:

> As scientific understanding has grown, so our world has become dehumanized. Man feels himself isolated in the cosmos, because he is no longer involved in nature and has lost his emotional "unconscious identity" with natural phenomena. These have slowly lost their symbolic implications … His contact with nature has gone, and with it has gone the profound emotional energy that this symbolic connection supplied.[36]

Jung explains his work in a potently cosmological and symbolic sense.

> Since the stars have fallen from heaven and our highest symbols have paled, a secret life holds sway in the unconscious. This is why we have a psychology today, and why we speak of the unconscious. All this would be quite superfluous in an age or culture that possessed symbols … Our unconscious, on the other hand, hides living water … "the heart glows," and a secret unrest gnaws at the roots of our being.[37]

Could we understand symbol here in its original sense in which God and man commune together? According to Scott,

> The symbol is the immanent expression of the Divine. Through participation in both the sensible and the

metaphysical orders of ontological Existence the symbol acts as the vehicle by which the human may be lead back to the Divine.[38]

Jung presents his understanding of this in terms of the psyche. Main proposes that there is a continuum of consciousness and reality, physical, psychic and spiritual which is "an aspect both of every individual person and of the world as it exists independently of any individual person."[39] This continuum is

a kind of spectrum: from physical to psychic to spiritual – is characterized by increasing subtlety of 'substance' and operation and consequently also by increasing difficulty of observation and quantification.[40]

Nevertheless, Jung was acutely aware of spirit and deemed manifestation of spirit as

characterized by numinosity, with all the qualities implicit in this term: otherness, awefulness, overpoweringness, urgency, fascination – in general, a distinctive prerational and transrational emotional charge.[41]

The workings of the spirit are compared with "its capacity for repatterning or restructuring contents within the fields of the psychic and physical"[42] as in intuitive or creative action. Jung accepts the terms matter, psyche and spirit and uses them all. However, he writes of "the relative validity of the realistic standpoint ... or of the idealistic standpoint ... ; I would only like to unite these extreme opposites by ... the psychological standpoint."[43]

Jung says, "We are in truth so wrapped about by psychic images that we cannot penetrate at all to the essence of things external to ourselves. All our knowledge consists of the stuff of the psyche which, because it alone is immediate, is superlatively real."[44] He is therefore locating psyche or soul as the only mode whereby news from the worlds of spirit and matter become conscious for us. In this sense, we may see him re-animating the idea of the role of the soul, as mediator between matter and spirit in the hermetic world; joining the two perspectives, the realistic and idealistic standpoints and also in a sense uniting the two functions of the human brain, as described by McGilchrist. Jung proposes the mind of man as uniting the opposites of the paradoxical world using symbol.

> How else could it have occurred to man to divide the cosmos, on the analogy of day and night, summer and winter, into a bright day-world and a dark night-world peopled with fabulous monsters, unless he had the prototype of such a division in himself, in the polarity between the conscious and the invisible and unknowable unconscious?[45]

He further says that "unequivocal statements can be made only in regard to immanent objects; transcendent ones can be expressed only by paradox"[46] and this matters because:

> The paradox is one of our most valuable spiritual possessions, while uniformity of meaning is a sign of weakness. Hence a religion becomes inwardly impoverished when it loses or waters down its paradoxes; but their multiplication enriches because only the paradox comes anywhere near to comprehending the fullness of life. Non-ambiguity and non-contradiction are one-sided and thus unsuited to express the incomprehensible.[47]

An awareness of living in a paradoxical world can be uncomfortable and the process of moving to appropriate lived relationship with it can be healing but can also pose major difficulties:

One should not underestimate the demands and the hazards involved in pursuing one's true personality. One is liable to encounter personal resistance or collective disapproval. And one never knows what the unconscious will produce, nor are there any guarantees of either success or return ... most of us are either called to it by some overwhelming summons or driven to it by some disturbing experience of suffering.[48]

Suffering for the ego, as it faces its shadow and is forced to undergo a kind of death in life, can become a form of psychoanalytic initiation.

The path of healing developed by Jung is based on a one-to-one therapeutic encounter, not unlike the divinatory encounter of *theoros* and *hermeios* as described by Cornelius[49] with the dream as the oracular and symbolic statement to be interpreted. Jung also worked with visualisation and took advice from divinatory resources such as the *I Ching*. His fascination with astrology is well known, although the outcome firmly locates astrology in the world of tricksterish symbolism, rather than materialist science, as Maggie Hyde observes.[50,51]

The symbolic attitude is an area of overlap between Jung and astrological practice. However, few astrologers today want to present themselves to the world as diviners or oracle interpreters. Like Jung, they would wish to present their work as founded on reason and science. Jung always affirmed that his work was based on empirical science, but for astrologers, in the present time, this is not an option. As Hyde says:

Divination has no public place and we would not expect our leaders to make known the omens before embarking on wars or other national enterprises. Whatever great men do in private, it remains publicly unacceptable to have a US President throw the *I Ching*, follow a dream or listen to an astrologer, as the stir over Ronald and Nancy Reagan's astrological advisor readily revealed. Jung lamented that even eastern cultures had stopped divining about affairs of state.[52]

Hyde says that it is not a simple matter of turning symbols into signs. In Ficino's terms, this process simply generates "silly similitudes". Jung is with Ficino on this point, that a symbol is dependent on the "consciousness of the one considering it".[53] Ficino speaks about *judicio* or judgement, and the quality of the judgement depends upon the personal maturity, wisdom and experience of the astrologer. Likewise, astrologers cannot simply stand aside and let symbol speak without an awareness of their own participation and the way the symbol affects them. Like psychologists, projection may be at work or the 'secret mutual connivance' identified by Jung[54] in his astrological experiments.

No one has done more than Liz Greene to bring about the marriage of Jungian analysis and astrological symbolism and bring them to the attention of the public. Given the poor status of astrology at the outset of her project, she has certainly enhanced its fascination for myriads of students and practitioners. Jungian astrology is now seen as a major strand within the contemporary astrological current. However, this has not protected these astrologers from sometimes adopting a simplistic and deterministic approach to their thinking about the subject. Hyde undertakes an analysis of Greene's own descriptions of her way of proceeding and finds that core astrological craft and technique can be lacking.[55] Ficino urges us to use both intuition and technique in our work. For Liz Greene it looks as though the symbolic imagination sometimes takes flight, forgetting the technique.

The ultimate concern has to be the effect on the client, whether of astrologer or psychoanalyst, and sometimes, most persuasively, when the two work together. Delia Shargel, a transpersonal analyst working in a tradition that builds on Jung's work, is convinced that astrological symbolism can aid the self-awareness and healing of suffering because it helps us move beyond the internalized modern world view of separateness and alienation by making a deep, numinous connection with the cosmos, mirroring us right down to the minutiae of our daily lives and the inner workings of our souls[56]

In my own experience as an astrological practitioner, this often happens by the telling of a myth related to a planet that appears likely to be significant. Telling the myth is not, in itself, an interpretation but the client can be aroused by the relevance of the analogy with their own situation. They then reveal what is going on, assisting the astrologer in moving, as Cornelius puts it, from the speculative to the realised interpretation.[57]

Shargel associates the healing capacity of this kind of work with the idea that astrological symbols are "*multivalent*, capable of expressing themselves in a multitude of ways while remaining consistent with a central archetypal core of meaning."[58] In this approach the symbol retains enough complexity to continue to function. However, as Ficino found, the native or astrological subject also has the capacity to make creative choices about how to live his life. Shargel says that, as a result of astrological insights, her client was able to choose:

> Different but still archetypally appropriate manifestations [and this] lets the archetypal energies at the core of the complex express themselves in more life-enhancing behaviour, thus promoting self-acceptance ... psychic energy is no longer as bound up in unconscious conflict. Furthermore, it is possible to recover from the activation of the complex more quickly by using the more conscious and compassionate parts of the psyche to help soothe underlying conflicts in a self-compassionate manner.[59]

Conclusions

This book proposes that hermeticism still has relevant ideas for us today in wrestling with a complex world and in responding to the problems we have created by adopting a left brain, objectivist and materialist focus. Clearly, astrology can adopt the hermetic approach demonstrated by Ficino. Many present-day astrologers could claim to be hermetic in the sense that they apply the principles of *sympatheia* to connect with the planets by way of myth, art, drama, food, medicine, music, incense and so on. Some would also claim a healing dimension to their practice, by combining psychology with astrology, or a spiritual dimension such as Kabbalistic astrology.[60] In all this, Ficino counsels that it is the judgement of the astrologer that counts. This depends upon their preparation, reverence and ability to combine and interpret the fruits of our two modes of thought.

The astrological practice envisaged by the hermetic texts would have been a form of divination.

Everywhere it occurs, divination involves complementary modes of cognition associated with primary process and secondary process thinking or knowing.[61]

> Diviners are specialists who use the idea of moving from a boundless to a bounded realm of existence in their practice ... [They] excel in insight, imagination, fluency in language, and knowledge of cultural traditions. During a divination, they construct usable knowledge from oracular messages. To do so, they link diverse domains of representational information and symbolism, with emotional or presentational experience.[62]

Although astrologers are often reluctant to accept the description of diviner, this is likely to be a consequence of the devaluation of these modes of thought in our time. We now begin to see that this devaluing is unhelpful, not simply to astrologers but in terms of a wider approach to human development.

Above all astrology is always a way of working with symbol. According to Scott,

> the symbol is the immanent expression of the Divine. Through participation in both the sensible and the metaphysical orders of ontological Existence the symbol acts as the vehicle by which the human may be lead back to the Divine.[63]

It can therefore be a means of "Re-membering" in the Platonic sense of anamnesia, leading to absolute knowledge. According to Snodgrass[64] symbols can be visual or spatial or found in myth, ritual or doctrine. The astrological symbol is founded on the cosmos itself which, according to Coleridge, is none other than

> one vast complex *Mythos*, or symbolic representation ... [and provides the] key for the return of the human to the Divine. This is to recognize Cosmic Existence as theophany ... the reflection of the Divinity in the mirror of created forms ... [and imaging the hermetic journey of the soul] 'The cosmos is not only the theatre wherein are reflected the Divine names and Qualities. It is also a crypt through which man must journey to reach the Reality beyond cosmic manifestation.[65]

Ultimately, Joseph Milne tells us:

> The way a culture views the cosmos determines the way it views human nature or understands itself. The two are inextricably bound together. If the cosmos is seen as essentially holy, and therefore as revelatory, as the religions and the poets have always seen it, then it is possible for the human soul to participate consciously in the providential destiny of the cosmic narrative. But if the cosmos is seen as an indifferent mechanism blindly hurtling to its eventual

extinction, then human nature will be seen likewise. It will be closed in upon itself and unable to find meaning outside its own alienated subjectivity, trying to invent itself from within, and likewise be unable to confer any blessings upon the earth or the heavens which the mystics regard as part of the true calling of humanity and which always closes Shakespeare's comedies.[66]

It is this holy cosmos that a hermetic astrology aspires to reveal.

Part 2

Journeys of Discovery:
Towards Creating a Play

Packing for the journey

It is an odd thing how the open space and instruction to "be creative" can cause all sense of creativity to flee. I did not feel even slightly creative at the outset of this journey. However, I did have some personal objectives that would inform it. For one thing the learning journal write-up was a reminder both of the journey so far and of unexplored territory. I wanted to know more about Ficino and his sources. I wanted to read the *Corpus Hermeticum*. What was it that Ficino had found there?

Here I will set out my starting thoughts, hopes and values. Then there are two journeys that follow. One is through the ideas gleaned from my sources, in particular the *Corpus Hermeticum*, Ficino's *Three Books on Life* and the thought of Ibn 'Arabi. The idea of the soul making a journey from the divine realm to earth and back became a play that would provide a container for much that I had in mind, this showing how some of the ideas were incorporated into the different roles. The next journey is through the production of the play itself, its rehearsals and performance. Finally, there is a moment to anchor the experience back to my starting point.

Because of the very openness of the task, I felt the need for some way of making choices. Packing for the journey involves sorting out how these choices would be made. Values are important to me for the way they inform behaviour. First and foremost is the value of unity as expressed by Ibn 'Arabi. This is an inclusive, both this and that, approach to philosophy and life. It is an antidote to the tyranny of certainty, of those who think there is only one truth and that all other "truths" must be suppressed. Not having a fixed or single truth requires a certain openness to experience. It implies not holding onto "the truth" but being open to the form in which truth will next reveal itself. There is a kind of drama involved in living this way.

Joe Landwehr takes the implications of unity one step further in *The Seven Gates of Soul*[1] and makes the point that our cosmology both profoundly affects our view of ourselves and our world and governs the effect we will have upon it. When Ficino says that we are made of body, soul and spirit and that spirit is omnipresent but requires animation and connection with body via the soul,[2] unity becomes a dynamic source of creation. I am reminded of *The Treatise on Being* "Every day He is in a business",[3] expressing this constant renewal of life as a work of the divine spirit.

There was a lovely serendipity for me when Dr Crystal Addey spoke in Edinburgh, about "Divination, Astrology and Ritual in the Ancient world".[4] She told us that, for people in the ancient world, "everything in the cosmos is connected and everything is full of soul and full of the gods." This view she said prevailed over a wide area, perhaps from India in the east, to France in the west and over at least 2,000 years, connecting the era of Plato with that of Marsilio Ficino. Dr Addey, in her talk, made the connection between this unified cosmos and astrology. This is another important piece of my luggage: the sense of astrology as a conversation with the gods.

Journeys of discovery in books and ideas

In my reading I found that my sources started to overlap and reference each other. All kinds of resonances and associations emerged as the work went along. In Part 3, the playscript contains the footnotes and references for the sources of props and ideas. Here I will say something about the main ideas I took from my sources and how they influenced the crafting of the play.

It was Gary Lachman's[5] discussion of the *Corpus Hermeticum* that brought home to me that the movement of the soul to earth is based on mutual love and desire. Lachman tells us "Now, having created the creator, and the creator having created a world, the first Nous, the Father, thought it good to create a being like himself to witness and enjoy this creation. So he brought forth

Man… [whom] the Father loved as he would his child".[6] Man sees the beauty of creation and wants to be a creator himself, so he "broke through the vault and stooped to look through the cosmic framework, thus displaying to lower nature the fair form of god. Nature smiled for love… [and] took hold of her beloved, hugged him all about and embraced him for they were lovers."[7]

This parallels the Koranic saying "I was a hidden treasure and I desired to be known, so I created the Universes that I might be known".[8,9] Love and beauty are fundamental to the whole of creation. These are hermetic ideas that permeated the world of Islamic Sufism, possibly from several directions. Peter Kingsley traces their movement between the ancient Greeks, the Egyptians and the Arabs and so into the thought of Suhrawardi "The Sheikh of the East" in the 12th century.[10] Gary Lachman tells us that "Suhrawardi spoke of an initiatic chain, a school of ancient adepts, comprising Hermes Trismegistus, Zoroaster, Pythagoras, Plato, and Plotinus".[11] Another route of transmission came via the Sabians of Harran. Harran was a refuge for scholars from Alexandria during a period of Christian persecution. When the Arabs arrived at Harran in the 9th century they demanded to know the religion of the city. The Harranians decided to adopt the name Sabians as these were a people protected by the Koran. Their prophet would be Hermes Trismegistus, whom they identified with the Moslem prophet Idris, and their sacred texts would be the hermetic books.[12] I sought inspiration for the play from some of the sources that are links in this initiatic chain.

The way Ficino understood this is described in his *Three Books on Life*. Ficino describes the permeation of the divine in the world, by way of the rays from the planets and stars,[13] drawing on the work of the Arabic scholar al-Kindi who, in turn, drew on the work of Plotinus. For al-Kindi, "The rays are emanations which act as the means whereby the stars and planets generate and influence … and it is compared to the light of the sun ceaselessly flowing from the One to the rest of the cosmos."[14] Ficino describes how the rays embed themselves in our world, for instance in gemstones. According to Ficino, the objects of this world that most purely express their planetary and divine origin, can be used by us as "baits and lures"[15] to attract divine properties into ourselves and our lives. Because the things of this world are linked to different planets we can assimilate the properties of the planets into ourselves by eating the right food and drinking the right wine.

Many traditions suggest that the soul forgets its source and past lives on arrival on earth and has to recover this lost knowledge. This is poignantly expressed by Rumi[16] in his poetry.[17] In *The Twenty-Nine Pages*,[18] a synopsis of Ibn 'Arabi's thought, the soul is presented as a knowing substance. This knowledge is recovered in the course of life, by way of the soul's recognition of its own spiritual attributes in the world around it. The world is therefore essential for our development.

In writing the play I had a dilemma as to how to express the way in which the soul forgets and how she returns. My practical solution was to anchor the soul's turning point to seeds, the gift of the Moon. The seeds stand for things that need nurturing. The Moon is associated with the mother and mothering, and thus the seeds represent all our hopes, loves, projects, new life. The soul comes from an eternal world, but the seeds are sown in a world of seasons. We are reminded of the passage in Ecclesiastes "To everything there is a season. A time for every purpose under heaven: A time to be born and a time to die; A time to plant, and a time to pluck what is planted".[19] The soul needs to come to terms with the earth's changing seasons and with death. The loss and distress over the dying plants echoes all our losses and griefs, hence Rumi's poem of the reed,[20] severed from its rushy bed. At this point in the play the soul feels cut off and longs to go "home". Her attention is drawn to the things she has brought with her from the planets. Maybe they can help her?

The soul returns to heaven and to wholeness in planet order, so next she meets Mercury. Mercury has a complex set of ideas and associations: here I was particulary inspired by the *Corpus*

Hermeticum, where the concept of mind is frequently mentioned. So what is this mind? The *Corpus Hermeticum* distinguishes between two zones of mental activity. One is limited and is referred to as reason.[21] The *Corpus Hermeticum* is completely damning about the people of reason. I interpreted this as possibly a reference to those who adopt a world view which is left hemisphere dominated. McGilchrist in *The Master and His Emissary* links the left brain exclusively with the emotion of anger.[22] In the *Corpus Hermeticum,* we are told "the many make philosophy obscure in the multiplicity of their reasoning"[23] "since their temperament is wilful and angry".[24] Reason is useful for the study of

> *arithmêtikê* and music and geometry. ... [However], pure philosophy that depends only on reverence for god should attend to these other matters only to wonder at the recurrence of the stars... in order to commend, worship and wonder at the skill and mind of god.[25]

"Those who do not do this suffer a vile migration unworthy of a holy soul".[26] It gets worse, for in the *Asclepius,* another hermetic text, we learn that if we fail to reverence the gods they will simply leave us. A materialist view might then be that nothing will happen, since there are no gods anyway. Not so says the *Asclepius:* on the contrary, all hell will be let loose. The grief and curse of Trismegistus in the *Asclepius* is very powerful: "how mournful when the gods withdraw from mankind! Only the baleful angels remain ..."[27, 28] This passage had a big impact on me. It may have felt real in the third century AD in Egypt, as the Christians sought to eliminate the old religion, but it feels even more potent now, as we conjure with the possibilities of earthly destruction by climate change.

The *Corpus Hermeticum* suggests that mind should have another quite different role, one concerned with divination and the myriad ways the gods communicate with us both through mind and through the world. From the *Corpus Hermeticum* I gave Mercury the words

Through mind, then, every living thing is immortal. ...
With this living thing alone does god converse, at night
through dreams and through omens by day, and through
them all, he foretells the future, through birds, through
entrails, through inspiration, through the oak tree, whereby
mankind also professes to know what has been, what is at
hand what will be.[29]

Dr Addey in her talk has confirmed that across the ancient
world, there was "Less separation between rational knowledge
and other forms of knowledge, such as intuition".[30] The *Corpus
Hermeticum* tells us that "humankind is divine in one part, in
another mortal, residing in a body." Those who honour both
sides of their nature receive "the prize, that is, of discharge and
release from worldly custody, of losing the bonds of mortality
so that god may restore us, pure and holy, to the nature of our
higher part, to the divine",[31] a sentiment that McGilchrist might
appreciate. I wanted Mercury to have gifts, symbols to represent
these ideas. The winding map of the labyrinth was one way of
indicating the indirect path of unreasoning perception, as well
as the twists and turns of our earthly lives. Clarity of perception
is indicated by the mirror, which requires to be cleaned so
that we can see ourselves with veracity. Dr Addey reminded us
of the words of Vettius Valens in his *Anthology:* "Once I had
experienced the divine and reverent contemplation of celestial
phenomena, I wished to cleanse my character of every kind of
vice and pollution and leave my soul immortal".[32] These ideas
meant Mercury was no longer simply a god of messages but the
path of divine wisdom.

Ibn 'Arabi identifies the heart as the organ of true knowledge.[33]
Since Venus is the goddess of love and all things desirable, she I
associated with the heart's desire. I was keen to try to integrate
Ibn 'Arabi's ideas of the different types of love somewhere into her
role. Ibn 'Arabi tells us that the lowest type of love seeks to possess
the beloved and in the process risks destroying the love object.

Love is essentially the cause of creation, and the aim of spiritual love is the "realisation of the essential unity of the lover and the Beloved."[34] Once again there seemed to be a matching duality in the expression of love and desire in the *Corpus Hermeticum*. The love of desire and possession seems to be associated with the people of reason for "they divert their attention to the pleasures and appetites of their bodies; and they believe that mankind came to be for such purposes."[35] Only those who "immersed themselves in mind participated in knowledge and became perfect people".[36]

Marsilio Ficino writes of the Sun as almost a second god. He is also versed in the different kinds of wines the Sun and Jupiter are associated with. I found his fondness for an uplifting tipple rather endearing, so gave the Sun some light, golden, wine.[37] The golden cup of the sun could symbolise a grail or a Ting as in the *I Ching*, a vessel of nourishment. Preparing a place to receive the spirit is a recurring theme at the Beshara School, thus, this simple item can be loaded with meaning and is a natural accompaniment to the wine.[38] In Kabbalah the vice or sin associated with the Sun is pride,[39, 40] so I allowed my soul to fall into the sin of pride on account of the major lessons learned from the Moon, Mercury and Venus. In more contemporary astrology Neptune has been associated with the hubris of the false guru. I was surprised how well the Sun fitted this role in the older cosmology.

As with Mercury and Venus, I found Mars to be a useful hook for quite divergent sets of ideas and behaviours. Symbolically, Mars could be the agent of anger as well as the agent of courage. Kupperman discusses the Platonic virtues and he shows that the virtue of courage is not rash or impulsive.[41] On the contrary the person of courage shows a steadfast quality, through knowledge of what is really to be feared. From Sahaja Yoga, the question and response "Who am I? I am not this body. I am the pure spirit" shed a light for me on this Martial knowledge and virtue. If I am not this body, what bodily fate can I fear in reality? Of course, Mars can express the anger of the people of reason, as well. However, my sense is that this would be seen by my sources as a misattribution of his power, which is to hold firmly to the life of the spirit, in whatever form it takes. Mars, in my play, is about actions rather than words, and his positive attributes are pointed out by Jupiter. Ficino[42] tells us that Jupiter has a tempering influence and this is shown by his intervention at a crucial stage in the play, when the soul is struggling to come to terms with Mars. Perhaps the tempering influence of Jupiter can be compared to that of salt, not dominating the taste of the food but selflessly bringing out its flavours.

For Saturn I opted for things that would evoke the confining disciplines of matter, space and time. On her descent from heaven, the soul first meets Saturn. Saturn indicates the advent of mortality by turning the soul's white or, as it turned out, silver cloak, into a black one. This cloak is reminiscent of the Mevlevi dervish's cloak of mortality, that is cast off in the course of the Sema or the ceremony of turning.[43] Ficino associates Saturn with deep study and learning.[44] This, for sure, is the way he gave positive form to his own Saturn, so what better than for Saturn to give the Soul the *Corpus Hermeticum* as a symbol of this aspect of his role. On the return journey, Saturn has the final planetary act of dismantling and disrobing. This kind of move begs a lot of questions about what has been integrated. Do we only really know when we die, or, as Ibn 'Arabi would urge, "die before you die"?[45] Are the planetary attributes converted into "himma", spiritual energy? At the end of the play, the effect of this stripping is that the soul recognises her place of origin and wholeness, as expressed through the lines of Rumi's poem, *The Soul of the World*.[46] Overall the play that was at first a patchwork of quotes and references, became, for me, a dense and colourful symbol.

The journey of making the play

I have never scripted a play before, or taken part in one, so when I realised my project would be a play with several parts, I knew I needed help. Angela Voss suggested that I put together planet profiles showing Ficino's "baits and lures". This enabled me to assemble relevant objects in a process of making the ideas tangible. There was a reflective process of expanding the objects to encompass the profile information and then eliminating many of them as being too unwieldly and not visual or relevant enough. For instance, Ficino's herbs and spices might have been presented in little colour wedding comfit bags. Ficino writes about how good it is to walk in the garden and smell the herbs, but fresh herbs were not in season. I thought of making a map of the herbs in my own garden, with their planetary associations, but could not manage this in the time.

I set about acquiring a costume. I saw myself as the soul and bought myself a white outfit, indicating the purity of white light, pointing to the soul's place of origin and return. I also wanted a cloak. How evocative cloaks can be! Lots of my childhood heroes, Zorro, El Cid or the three Musketeers, had cloaks to swish about and look dramatic in.

I wanted to rehearse and gave thought to where and how to do this. At first I imagined the play acted out in a labyrinth, such as the grass labyrinth at Canterbury. Use of the grass labyrinth seemed impractical in December. Nevertheless, for a rehearsal in Edinburgh, I found a labyrinth in my local church. The labyrinth coordinator was happy for me to have free access on a Wednesday and was keen to see what I was up to.[47] In the end there were two rehearsals at the church. On the first occasion, I was buoyed up by the interest of my helpers and gained helpful suggestions for editing. The second time around was more of a dress rehearsal and I realised then that my props needed further editing. They had to act as clear symbols linked to the planet unambiguously. They also had to be small and portable.

From the rehearsals, I saw scope to develop the play as a workshop with the chance for everyone to reflect on the experience of taking on a role. Do people connect more strongly with one role than another? Does this resonate with their natal or progressed chart? Could it be an experiential kind of astrological teaching tool? Do the ideas have wider consequences for the way we relate to ourselves, each other and the world?

For the performance in Canterbury I was impressed by how positive and helpful everyone was. All were willing to be involved and some positively revelled in their role. There was a certain serendipity in the allocation of roles to people who matched the planets, or who, like all actors, were able to find the relevant qualities in their nature. After so much preparation it seemed to be all over in a flash.

Souvenirs from the journey

So what did I learn from all this? For one thing, the importance of making knowledge tangible. The colours, images and props vividly brought out the different personalities of the planets. In hindsight, I noticed that Judith (the Earth) had chosen to wear a rainbow garment, illustrating the idea that the earth contains all the colours, imaging them each in a distinctive way that is not apparent in the white light of heaven. This physical knowledge is complemented by the importance of acting it out. Insights revealed in performance would not have surfaced purely from reading. Ideas for further projects, whether by way of workshops or exploring herbs and foods, or the links with other traditions, such as the Hindu chakras and the Sephira of the Kabbalah, constantly surfaced. The *Corpus Hermeticum* offered a number of powerful lessons and, with its emphasis on the need to care for the mind, seemed in some ways surprisingly modern, potent and relevant. The business of working with others introduced a sense of vulnerability for me. I depended on them. It was also a joy. They all brought so much to the table and many revealed hidden strengths.

Going back to my starting objectives, the drama and uncertainty as to how each enactment would go, created a dynamic uncertainty. We had to live and adapt in the moment. The play expresses unity in diversity by virtue of being one thing, albeit stitched from different pieces. The action becomes a kind of crucible in which a new whole can emerge. This will be different with each performance and each group of performers. Unity of spirit satisfies my ecological aspiration. There is no need of a "green" or earth-centred spirituality here. If, as Plato and Ibn 'Arabi affirm, the spirit or the divine is everywhere, and if, as Ficino suggests, the role of the soul is to unite and enliven matter with spirit, then our role in the world is clear. Not use, not exploitation, but the bringing out of life and beauty through love and being second creators like the demiurge, thereby encompassing the macrocosm in the microcosm.

Part 3

Playscript:
The Journey of the Soul

The Journey of the Soul

Dramatis Personae	Props and colours
Narrator	Black, dark or neutral colour
Soul	Cloak and white clothes
Saturn	Grey or dusky colours Props: book, a container for the props the soul will carry
Jupiter	Purple or other rich warm colours
Mars	Red Props: red ribbon, stage knife
Sun	Gold colours or light sparkly things Props: golden chalice, ribbon and sparkling golden wine
Venus	The colours of grass or spring flowers Props: bronze coloured willow pattern plate, pomegranate
Mercury	Mixed light metallic or electric blue colours Props: origami fortune teller, map, mirror, ribbon
Moon	Pale colours, white or silver Props: seeds, water, ribbon
Earth	Any colours associated with the fruitfulness of the earth Props: fruit, flowers

The Journey of the Soul

*[Each planet has something to give the Soul. Some of these things
will simply be left on the Earth. At the end of the play, Saturn
will remove any of these gifts the Soul happens to still be wearing
or carrying. Planets and the Earth should preferably be wearing
colours suitable to their role.]*

Narrator　Now attend! Here we will disclose to you the
meaning of the creation of the cosmos. The meaning
of the creation of the soul.

God says "I was hidden treasure and I loved to be
known, so I created the universes that I might be
known".[1] Hear how this came to be.

"The mind who is god, being androgyne and existing
as life and light, by speaking, gave birth to a second
mind, a craftsman, who as god of fire and spirit,
crafted seven governors: they encompass the sensible
world in circles, and their government is called fate."

"Mind the father of all, who is life and light, gave
birth to a man like himself, whom he loved as
his own child. The man was most fair: he had his
father's image; and god, who was really in love with
his own form, bestowed on him all his craftworks.
And after the man had observed what the craftsman
had created with the father's help, he also wishes
to make some craftwork, and the father agreed to
this. Entering the craftsman's sphere, where he was
to have all authority, the man observed his brother's
craftwork; the governors loved the man, and each
gave a share of his own order."[2]

Soul　　　See the world of nature, how rich, how fair, how
beautiful it is. How I long to go there!

Earth	See the Soul of humankind in the form of the living god. See how this Soul is made to contain all the energy of the governors. Even now I see their form in the waters and their shadow upon all the land.[3] Come here for I long to embrace you.
Soul	I fly on wings of desire.
Narrator	So the Soul sets off in the direction of the Earth and first encounters Saturn.
Saturn	[Sternly] Wait! Not so fast, you wish to take on bodily form. Do you know what you are doing? Once born the soul does not remember her ancient abode and birth place, since she is wrapped in the slumber of this world, like a star covered by clouds.[4]
Soul	How can I forget, when I am the bearer of pure Spirit, the mind of God the Father?
Saturn	For sure you will forget. Your way home is through me. Take from me now my gifts for your safety and protection. First take on a colour more suited to your earthly form.
Narrator	Saturn then removes the Soul's cloak and turns it black side out, before tying it back around the Soul. Saturn then presents the Soul with a basket and a book saying:
Saturn	And take this, for you are a container and must carry in your person all the gifts the governors will give you. And most importantly take this book, for nothing is more godlike than mind. Blessed is the soul full of mind. Therefore, study well and attend to the condition of your mind.[5]
Soul	Thank you father Saturn.
Saturn	Be mindful, be sure that you obey!

Soul	I will attend and thank you for everything.
Narrator	The Soul sets off, somewhat burdened by the gifts of Saturn. She continues until hailed by Jupiter.
Jupiter	Come now, come to me next, for I am she through whom all good things come to humankind. *[Opens her arms to embrace and reassure the Soul]*
Soul	Jupiter thank you, I am so glad to meet you.
Jupiter	From me you must have three of the five things you need for the return. They are patience, trust and certainty and are called the rope of God.[6] Fear not, for from Mars you will gain resolution and from Mercury, veracity. Therefore, let your heart be light, for remember God is love. When love of God waxes in your heart, beyond any doubt God has love for you.[7] Here is something that will help you to remember me.
Narrator	And Jupiter wraps a purple cloth around the Soul so that the Soul takes on some of Jupiter's own colour.
Soul	Oh Jupiter you speak wisely, never does the lover seek without being sought by the beloved. I will hold firmly to patience, trust and certainty, knowing that love in my heart.
Narrator	So the Soul moves on with a greater sense of confidence until confronted by Mars, who steps out across the path, blocking the way.
Mars	Halt, who goes there!
Soul	It is I, the Soul of the world.
Mars	Hah you will need a few things from me to take on your way! Take courage and bravery.
Soul	Why am I to be a dashing hero then?

Mars   You will be a hero if you are brave but you will only be a fool if you are foolhardy.

Soul   So what is the difference? How will I know which is which?

Mars   See here *[holds up the knife for all to see]* my knife is for discrimination. I stride forward undeterred by matters of no consequence. I ask you to discern in your mind what is really to be feared and what is not.

Soul   But the world is beautiful. Are there things to be feared in it?

Mars   Some will tell you so, but mostly this comes from fear itself. In reality you are nothing but a pure spirit, an immortal. Therefore, be resolute on your path. Here, take this to remind yourself of me.

Narrator   And here Mars presents the Soul with a red ribbon signifying courage. The Soul is rather pleased with the ribbon having no idea as yet, of its association with blood.

Soul   Thank you. I shall remain steadfast in the knowledge of the Spirit.[8] Now where? And what is that brightness in my eyes that competes with the pure light of God?

Sun   Here Soul come to me for "the entire soul ... dwells most of all in the heart and in the Sun."[9] I give you joy and the gift of being heart centred[10] With my gifts you will always know and speak your truth and be welcome in the best company.

Soul   Oh Sun what a blessing you are!

Sun   Now to remember me you must have wine *[Offers golden sparkling wine]*[11] for, as the poet says
        "I drank glass after glass of love; neither did the wine

finish, nor my thirst."[12] And wine is useless without a
cup. *[Hands a golden goblet]*

Soul I drink to your radiant majesty. Honour and grace is
yours. Thank you Helios, Thank you Apollo.

Narrator Thus fortified and cheered the Soul continues on
her way to meet Venus who will teach her lessons in
love. The poet says
"Regard Earth and Heaven as endowed with
intelligence, since they do the work of intelligent beings.
Unless these twain taste pleasure from one another,
why are they creeping together like sweethearts ...
The body desires green herbs and running water,
because its origin is from those;
The soul desires Life and the Living One, because its
origin is the Infinite Soul."[13]

Venus Welcome child of innocence. Your love of beauty has
sent you on this journey. Your beloved is the Earth
who longs to embrace you. I am the desire that gives
your heart wings.

Soul You mean heaven and earth are meant to be united?

Venus Of course.

Soul For there to be love there have to be two beings, each
the lover, each the beloved? Does that mean you
have two gifts to give me?

Venus Why yes, two souvenirs of love. Guard them
carefully. You think you know love now but their
meaning will be all the clearer when you arrive.

Soul Oh please do let me see.

Narrator So here Venus holds up a copper coloured willow
pattern plate and tells the Soul the story of the two
lovers.

Venus   Do you see the two love birds flying in the sky? And do you see the young woman and the man, two lovers?

Soul   Yes – I do.

Venus   On Earth their story will be yours as well. But wait you wanted two gifts. Here is another token of the taste of love. *[Gives the Soul a pomegranate]*

Soul   A yellow fruit … with many luscious pink fruits in it.

Venus   On Earth you will taste them by and by.

Soul   Oh they are sure to taste good.

Narrator And with this, Venus wraps a cloth with the colours of spring flowers, around the Soul, so that she takes on the colours of Venus herself.

Soul   Thank you, now I must be on my way.

Narrator Next the Soul should meet Mercury but this goddess is busy playing with a toy.

Mercury *[Mercury is playing with an origami fortune teller]* Hi, hey wait a minute. Don't you want to play a game? Look, it's fun. I'll show you how it works. You see these four here are for earth, air, water and fire. You pick one and then I open it up … Now choose a number between 1 and 8.

Soul   Seven.

Mercury *[Opens the fortune teller]* See here, under seven, it says "practice meditation", so that's what you have to do. Cultivate and calm your mind.

Soul   Oh, I will need to practice that. Have you got any more games or puzzles?

Mercury Oh yes, how about this? *[Mercury produces a map/ labyrinth picture with a flourish]*

Soul   What is it?

Mercury It's a map. It will show you where to go.

Soul   A map to tell me where to go – I wish I'd had that earlier.

Mercury Put it away, keep it safe. And here's something else.

Soul   What's that?

Mercury Here, a mirror, you need to polish it, then it will show you the truth. This is for veracity. When you look in a clear mirror you will always know who you really are.

Narrator The Soul polishes the mirror and looks in it for the truth. Just like the map, the Soul finds the mirror somewhat baffling. Meantime Mercury ties a coloured ribbon to the Soul.

Soul   Well thank you Mercury. Which way is it now?

Mercury Got your map? *[Soul looks at the map and the path in complete confusion]*

Mercury This way *[Mercury points the soul towards the audience. Soul proceeds in the wrong direction.]*

Moon   *[The Moon actively looks about to find the Soul]* Oh poor little Soul, are you lost dear? Come here to me. You're nearly home you know.

Soul   Oh mother Moon, how lovely to see you. Is it far to go? Can you help me?

Moon   Here child, let me give you a hug. You will soon be there. Let me give you a few things you will need on Earth. *[Gives the Soul a pack of seeds and a bottle of water]* Here are seeds, these are for life and living things. It is for this that you wish to join with the Earth. And here is some water too. This is the source

	of all life and comes under my governance. Your seeds will need earth and water to grow, cherish them and they will feed you well.
Soul	Oh wonderful, of course I will do my best. And now which way?
Moon	Follow my light and it will take you home. *[Moon ties a white ribbon to the Soul, who leaves for Earth]*
Soul	This is Earth, how delightful!
Earth	Welcome this is your home. It's time to explore.
Narrator	And so the Soul is born. She forgets her journey and all the gifts she has been given. None of this matters at first, because everything is a toy and a thing of wonder to her. Eagerly the Soul explores each thing she finds.
Soul	These flowers are beautiful. I wish I could make some more.
Earth	You can, did you not bring some seeds with you? *[Soul is astonished, looks in her basket and draws out the pack of seeds]*
Earth	Yes, that's right, you can plant those and they will grow into flowers, herbs or even trees.
Narrator	Now the Soul is in the Garden of Eden, delighting in the world and in growing things. However, she is unprepared for the cycle of life. She sees the seeds she has planted grow, flourish and die. Full of distress she tries to resuscitate the dead things.
Soul	Oh no, what is wrong? All that is beautiful, all I have loved, is fading and decaying. Will I be all alone here? Is there nothing to be done?
Earth	No child, do not say so. You were sent here for a

purpose. Why are you carrying this heavy load? You came with seeds and water for fruitfulness. Now it is the winter of our days, what else did you bring?

Narrator   At this point the Soul notices that she is burdened with things she does not understand. She takes out each item, looks at it and discards it in disgust, not realising its purpose. The wine she enjoys for a moment of pleasure but then, even that is gone.

Soul   Oh, why have I come here, oh weary, useless, lonely waste of days.

Narrator   And so the Soul reaches a place known by many before. As the poet says: "Listen to the reed how it tells a tale, complaining of separations – Saying, "Ever since I was parted from the reed bed, my lament has caused man and woman to moan … "In our woe the days (of life) have become untimely: our days' travel hand in hand with burning griefs."[14]

Soul   Oh what a joyless song I hear. Is this all that is left to me here, grief?

Narrator   The journey of return starts from the lowest of the low.

Soul   The journey of return? What is this return? Where shall I return to? If this is not my home, then where?

Narrator   The entire cosmos is free from change, but its parts are all subject to change. Nothing, however, is corruptible or destroyed … Life is not birth but awareness, and change is forgetting, not death. Since this is so, all are immortal – matter, life, spirit, soul, mind – of which every living thing is constituted.[15]

Soul   Oh, Moon mother, what does this mean? Must everything die that is in the world? Must I be aware of everything and remember everything?

Moon   Do not be afraid child, your first lessons concern
        the cycle of life and the depth of your own feeling.
        Without this feeling, how would you know love?
        Without love how would you connect with the Life
        of the world? Do not be like those whose hearts are
        in a sheath. Tears soften the heart and this will take
        you on your next steps. Remember your home, the
        Earth, and I are always with you on the journey of
        return.

Soul   Oh, I feel a bit better for knowing that. And I have
        come here with all these things. I guess I had better
        try to find out what they are for. Maybe if I keep
        a clear head, I won't have to suffer these feelings of
        despair so much. *[Rummages through the gifts and
        finds the map and mirror of Mercury. Holds up the
        map]* Oh my, I don't think I shall ever understand
        this.

Mercury Do not shut up the soul in the body and say I
        cannot do this or that ... to will to know is the easy
        way to the good and as you journey, the good will
        meet you everywhere and when you least expect it.[16]

Soul   But what is this knowing? I thought I knew
        something when I planted and watered the seeds. I
        didn't know then that they would die or what that
        meant.

Mercury In what comes to be and has come to be, there is
        nothing where god is not, nothing beyond him.[17]
        Through mind, then, every living thing is immortal
        ... With this living thing alone does god converse,
        at night through dreams and through omens by
        day, and through them all, he foretells the future,
        through birds, through entrails, through inspiration,
        through the oak tree, whereby mankind also

86

professes to know what has been, what is at hand what will be.[18] But do not confuse mind with reason. The people of reason alone, their temperament is wilful and angry, they feel no awe of things that deserve to be admired; they divert their attention to the pleasures and appetites of their bodies; and believe that mankind came to be for such purposes.[19]

Soul　　And it is not so? Mind must rule reason. But how can we rule the mind?

Mercury　Only when the mind is still and ceases reasoning and in response to the heart's desire, does the true dream come.

Soul　　The mind must be still. Well perhaps if I meditate every day, my mind will be a bit more still. But I am not too sure about the heart's desire. Feelings have hurt me before. I'm sure I used to know something about love. How I wish I could love and be loved without being hurt.

Venus　　Why child don't you know that love is the whole cause of creation. The poet says "Love is a boundless ocean, in which the heavens are but a flake of foam./ Know that all the wheeling heavens are turned by waves of Love:"[20]

Soul　　Venus that's very beautiful but how can I know this love, feel this love?

Venus　　Why you must open your heart. When you came to this world you saw beauty on every side. You can see this again through the eye of the heart. The poet says

"My heart has become capable of every form: it is a pasture for gazelles and a convent for Christian monks,

87

And a temple for idols and the pilgrim's Ka'ba and
the tables of the Tora and the book of the Koran.
I follow the religion of Love: whatever way Love's
camels take, that is my religion and my faith."[21]

Soul   And can I have this love simply by opening my heart
to all the beauty in the world?

Venus   Love will be yours when you are the loving servant of
beauty. For in natural love the object is sacrificed for
the lover, who seeks only to possess it but in spiritual
love you will love and serve beauty in yourself and in
the world, through the heart of God.[22]

Soul   Oh that sounds wonderful. Love will be everything
and everywhere. *[During this next speech all gods
except Mars and the Sun lose interest and turn away
from the Soul. The Sun is unimpressed and Mars
is furious.]* Oh see now how much progress I am
making here. Now I understand the meaning of
life and death, the world of feelings; the purpose
of the mind; the delights of the heart. Surely, this
is happiness and fulfilment. And since I see these
things everywhere, I have become a seer and it is
time to share what I have learned. Oh Sun, oh
second god, the very mirror of the one God, is it not
so? Am I not theos?

Sun   *[Unimpressed]* Even so.

Soul   I will be a teacher, an avatar, loving and wise, the
source of wisdom and beauty in the world, to the
praise of god. Is it not so?

Sun   *[Unimpressed]* Even so.

Soul   Ah joy, what better life could there be but to spread
love and wisdom throughout the world.

Mars   *[Confronts the Soul]* Until you die!

Soul   *[Trying to ignore Mars]* Ah, of course, all that lives must die. But I am a fount of wisdom and I will be protected since I do God's work. *[Mars stands tall, dynamic and threatening]*

Mars   Until you die! Die now, die at once, cursed wretch! You think you will make your fancy wisdom, your love, into a marketable product. See what I care for that! *[Soul wakes up to the danger and collapses in terror]*

Soul: Angels and ministers of grace defend me. The world descends into the chaos of war under this god's hand. *[Mars glares at individual members of the audience, threatening them at a distance during this speech]*

Narrator   "How mournful when the gods withdraw from mankind! Only the baleful angels remain to mingle with humans, seizing the wretches and driving them to every outrageous crime – war, looting, trickery and all that is contrary to the nature of souls. Then neither will the earth stand firm nor the sea be sailable; stars will not cross heaven, nor will the course of stars stand firm in heaven. Every divine voice will grow mute in enforced silence. The fruits of the earth will rot; the soil will no more be fertile; and the very air will droop in gloomy lethargy."[23]

Soul   Oh guide, oh saving grace, oh that it will not be this way! Show me, please, what, if anything, can I do in the face of this god's wrath?

Narrator   You must remember why god made man with a dual nature. In order to take care of the world "God shapes mankind from the nature of soul and of body, from the eternal and the mortal, in other words, so that the living being so shaped can prove adequate to both its beginnings, wondering at heavenly beings and worshipping them, tending earthly beings and governing them."[24]

Soul   You mean all this violence and disaster will fall upon a world that lacks reverence for the gods?

Narrator   Indeed so.

Soul   And where should I begin?

Narrator   Begin with reverence for the sun. *[Sun grandly and quietly turns at this]*

Narrator   For the sun illuminates the other stars, not so much by the intensity of its light as by its divinity and holiness. The sun is indeed a second god … governing all things and shedding light on all that are in the world, ensouled and soulless.[25]

Soul   *[Gets up and anxiously searches for the solar gifts]* Reverence the sun. Oh where is that with which I may do the sun honour? Oh look here, golden wine and a golden cup. Oh solar lady please do me favour and accept this libation?

Sun   *[Graciously]* Your gift is welcome. I for my turn, sustain your heart and give to you the gift of fire. Only a soul with this gift of fire can truly be a creator.[26]

Soul   Dear solar lady, your grace gives me hope. I will surely honour you. But look all you gods, how threatening Mars is. The tribute of Mars is surely blood, fear and panic. What should we do? *[In response all gods look back at the Soul]*

Earth   Remember Mars has given you gifts too. The gifts of discernment and fearlessness for fighting the fight of reverence. Knowing the divine and doing wrong to no person is the fight of reverence.[27]

Soul   I do wish to fight this fight of reverence but I am
            afraid. Oh gods who will help me now?

Jupiter   Have patience, have trust, have certainty in your
            purpose. Remember Mars also gave you resolution.
            *[Mars stands proudly but also watchfully during this
            next speech, waiting for the Soul's response]*

Jupiter   "Until one is committed, there is hesitancy, the
            chance to draw back, always ineffectiveness.
            Concerning all acts of initiative (and creation),
            there is one elementary truth, the ignorance of
            which kills countless ideas and splendid plans: that
            the moment one definitely commits oneself, the
            providence moves too. A whole stream of events
            issues from the decision, raising in one's favour
            all manner of unforeseen incidents, meetings and
            material assistance, which no man could have dreamt
            would have come his way."[28] When you make this
            commitment then Mars becomes your friend.

Soul   I see there is no way out but through. To abandon
            the path is to suffer a living death and be tortured
            by the fire of the Sun; the judgement of what might
            have been. The path of life follows Ariadne's thread
            through the dark; now caring for the spirit of love
            and beauty in the world, now cherishing it directly
            in the gods; owning the presence and the gifts of all
            the gods. Oh Jupiter thank you for this wise teaching
            of yours. Show me now, am I truly reverencing all
            the gods?

Jupiter   There is one more lord you must honour before you
            are home, the guardian of the seventh heaven, the
            watcher at the gate, to him you must surrender true

gifts. Seek them now.

*[Soul finds the book and basket and starts reading
assiduously; as she does so she attracts Saturn's attention]*

Soul   My, what weighty words are here, secrets of life, keys
to the life everlasting.

Saturn   Words alone are not enough. Now you must
surrender all you have been given. Only the
judgement of the heart will serve. Give up all your
artefacts.

Narrator   And at this Saturn begins to gently take and set down
all the robes and colours, the basket and all its contents
from the Soul. Not even the learning acquired in long
years on Earth will serve the Soul now.

Saturn   Now we will see if you have become white light.

Narrator   So Saturn takes the Soul's cloak, turns it silver side
out and puts it back on the Soul. All the planets
watch the Soul as she remembers her true identity.

Soul   I have circled awhile with the nine Fathers in each
Heaven.
For years I have revolved with the stars in their signs
I receive my nourishment from God, as a child in
the womb;
Man is born once, I have been born many times.
Clothed in a bodily mantle, I have busied myself
with affairs,
And often have I rent the mantle with my own
hands.
I have passed nights with ascetics in the monastery,
I have slept with infidels before the idols in the
pagoda.
I am the pangs of the jealous, the pain of the sick …
Never did the dust of mortality settle on my skirt O

dervish! …

O son, I am not Shams-i Tabriz, I am the pure Light.
If thou seest me,
Beware! Tell not anyone what thou hast seen![29]

[All company face the audience and bow]

References

Books and Journals

Addey, C., 2014. *Divination and Theurgy in Neoplatonism: Oracles of the Gods.* 1st ed. Farnham: Ashgate Publishing Ltd.

Allen, M.J.B., 1995. *Plato's Third Eye: Studies in Marsilio Ficino's Metaphysicsand its Sources.* Aldershot/Brookfield: Ashgate.

'Arabi, Ibn., 1976. *"Whoso Knoweth Himself"*. Sherborne near Cheltenham: Beshara Publications.
—1978. *The Tarjuman al-Ashwaq.* London: Theosophical Publishing House.
—1998. *The Twenty-Nine Pages.* 1st ed. Cheltenham: A Beshara Publication.
—n.d. *Kernel of the Kernel.* Sherborne, nr Cheltenham: Beshara Publications.

Brockbank, J., 2003. Planetary signification from the second century until the present day. *Culture and Cosmos,* 7(2), pp.37-62.

Burckhardt, T., 1977. *Mystical Astrology According to Ibn 'Arabi.* Aldsworth: Beshara Publications.

Copenhaver, B.P., 2000. *Hermetica.* Cambridge: Cambridge University Press.

Corbin, H., 1971. *En Islam: aspects spirituels et phioosophiques.* Paris: Gallimard.

Cornelius, G., 2003. *The Moment of Astrology: Origins in Divination.* Bournemouth: TheWessex Astrologer Ltd.
—2009. *Field of Omens: A Study in Inductive Divination.* University of Kent.

Dyer, R.D., 2000. *Jung's Thoughts on God: Religious Depths of the Psyche.* York Beach(Maine): Nicolas-Hays.

Ecclesiastes, 1982. Holy Bible. Nashville: Thomas Nelson Publishers.

Ficino, M., 1975. *The Letters of Marslio Ficino.* London: Shepheard-Walwyn.
—1996. *Meditations on the Soul.* 6 ed. London: Shepheard-Walwyn.

—1998. *Three Books on Life.* Binghampton (New York): Society of Renaissance Studies.
—2016. On the Nature of Love: Ficino on Plato's Symposium. London: Shepherd-Walwyn Ltd.

Garin, E., 1990. *Astrology in the Renaissance: The Zodiac of Life.* London: Penguin Group.

Goodrick-Clarke, N., 2008. *The Western Esoteric Traditions.* Oxford: Oxford University Press.

Halevi, Z. b. S., 1991. The Way of Kabbalah. Bath: Gateway Books.
—1986. *The Anatomy of Fate.* Bath: Gateway Books.

Hyde, M., 1992. *Jung and Astrology.* London: The Aquarian Press.

Jung, C.G., 1964. *Man and His Symbols.* London: Aldus Books, Jupiter Books.
—1969. *Collected Works, Vol 8.* 2 ed. London: Routledge and Kegan Paul Ltd.
—1971. *C.G. Jung: Psychologicl Reflections.* 2nd ed. London: Routledge & Kegan Paul Ltd..

Kingsley, P., 1993. Poimandres: The Etymology of the Name and the Origins of the Hermetica. *Journal of the Warburg and Courtauld Institutes,* Volume 56, pp.1-24.
—2009. Paths of the Ancient Sages: A Pythagorean History. *Rosicrucian Digest,* pp.2-9.

Kupperman, J. S., 2013. Living Theurrgy. London: Avalonia.

Lachman, G., 2011. *The Quest for Hermes Trismegistus.* Edinburgh: Floris Books.
—2015. *The Secret Teachers of the Western World.* New York: Penguin.

Landwehr, J., 2004. *The Seven Gates of Soul.* Abilene: Ancient Tower Press.

Main, R., 2007. *Revelations of Chance: Synchronicty as Spiritual Experience.* Albany, New York: State University of New York Press.

McGilchrist, I., 2009. *The Master and his Emissary: The Divided Brain and the Making of the Western World.* 1 ed. London: Yale University Press.

Milne, J., 2007. The Cosmic Sense. In: A. Voss & J. Hinson Lall, eds. *The Imaginal Cosmos: Astrology, divination and the sacred*. Canterbury: The University of Kent, pp.1-8.

Naydler, J., 2005. *Plato, Shamanism and Ancient Egypt*. Oxford: Abzu Press.
Rumi, 1978. *Rumi Poet and Mystic*. London: Unwin Paperbacks.
—1982. *The Mathnawi*. Cambridge: E.J.W. Gibb Memorial Trust.

Saif, L., 2015. *The Arabic Infleunces on Early Modern Occult Philosophy*. 1st ed. Basingstoke: Palgrave Macmillan.

Schlamm, L., 2007. Jung's Visionary Mysticism. In: A.H.L.J. Voss, ed. *The Imaginl Cosmos: Astrology, divination and the sared*. Canterbury: University of Kent, pp.75-93.

Scott, T., 2000. Understanding "Symbol". *Sacred Web*, 6 (Winter), pp.1-14.

Shargel, D., 2016. Psychological and Astrological Complexes: An evolving persepctive. *Archai: The Journal of Archetypal Cosmology*, Saturn and the Theoretical Foundations of an Emerging Discipline (5), pp.61-85.

Shaw, G., 2014. *Theurgy and the Soul: The Neoplatonism of Iamblichus*. 2 ed. Kettering(OH): Sophia Perennis.

Tedlock, B., 2001. Divination as a Way of Knowing: Embodiment, Visualisation, Narrative, and Interpretation. *Folklore*, Volume 112, pp.189-197.

Uzdavinys, A., 2005. *The Golen Chain: An Anthology of Platonic and Pythagorean Philosophy*. 1 ed. Bloomington(Indiana): World Wisdom Books.
—2014. *Philosophy and Theurgy in Late Antiquity*. 1 ed. Kettering, OH: Sophia Perennis.

Voss, A., 2000. The Astrology of Marsilio Ficino: Divination or Science?. *Culture and Cosmos*, 4(2), pp.29-45.
—2006. *Marsilio Ficino*. 1 ed. Berkeley: Noth Atlatic Books.
—2011. God or the Daemon: Platonic Astrology in a Christian Cosmos. *Temenos Review*, 19 September, Volume 14, pp.96-116.

Willis, R. & Curry, P., 2004. *Astrology, Science and Culture: Pulling Down the*

Moon. Oxford: Berg Publishers.

Young, P., 1982. Ibn 'Arabi. *Journal of the Muhyiddin Ibn 'Arabi Society,* Volume 1, pp.8-11.

Young, V., 2016. *The Sacred Embrace of Placebo,* Canterbury: unpublished masters thesis.

Websites and Talks

Addas, C., 2016. Muhyiddin Ibn 'Arabi Society.
Available at: http://www.ibnarabisociety.org.uk/articles/addas1.html
[Accessed 14 January 2016].

Addey, C., 2015. *Divination, Astrology adn Ritual in the Ancient World* Edinburgh: Scottish Astrological Association Ltd.

Anon., 2016. Available at: http://www.beshara.org/ [Accessed 14 January 2016].

Chapman, 2002. *System Failure.*
Available at: http://www.demos.co.uk/files/systemfailure.pdf
[Accessed 21 September 2016].

Chapman, J., 2012. *Home Affairs Committee. Drugs: Breaking the Cycle.*
Written evidence submitted by Professor Jake Chapman, Demos Associate (DP136).
Available at: http://www.publications.parliament.uk/pa/cm201213/cmselect/cmhaff/184/184we119.htm
[Accessed 21 September 2016].

Devi, S.M.N., 2016. online meditation.
Available at: http://www.onlinemeditation.org/meditation-class-6/the-true-self-heart-chakra/

Empedocles, 2016. *godreadscom*
Available at: http://www.goodreads.com/quotes/109200-god-is-a-circle-whose-center-is-everywhere-and-its
[Accessed 19 September 2016].

Laboure, D., 1994. *http://www.skyscript.co.uk/7bodies.html.*
Available at: http://www.skyscript.co.uk/7bodies.html
[Accessed 19 Septmber 2016].

Lee, M., 2016. Goethe Society of North America.
Available at: http://www.goethesociety.org/pages/quotescom.html
[Accessed 16 January 2016].

Moyers, B. & Campbell, J., 2013. *Ep.1: Joseph Campbell and the Power of Myth – 'The Hero's Adventure'.*
Available at: http://billmoyers.com/content/ep-1-joseph-campbell-and-the-power-of-myth-the-hero%E2%80%99s-adventure-audio/
[Accessed 18 September 2016].

Neitzsche, F., 1997. *Modern History Sourcebook:Nietzsche: Paable of the Madman.*
Available at: http://sourcebooks.fordham.edu/mod/nietzsche-madman.asp
[Accessed 21 September 2016].

Quran, 2009–11. *corpus.quran.*
Available at: http://corpus.quran.com/translation.jsp?chapter=41&verse=53
[Accessed 19 September 2016].

Shah, I. t., 1964. *Sacred Texts.*
Available at: http://www.sacred-texts.com/alc/emerald.htm
[Accessed 27 July 2016].

Tyas, H. W. J., 2010. *Jungia Analytic Praxis.com.*
Available at: http://www.jungiananalyticpraxis.com/individuation_lecture.htm
[Accessed 21 Septemer 2016].

Versluis, A., 2002. *Esoterica.*
Available at: http://www.esoteric.msu.ed/VolumeIV/Methods.htm
[Accessed 29 August 2016].

Endnotes

Part 1

Chapter 1

1. Addey, 2015
2. Copenhaver, 2000
3. McGilchrist, 2009
4. Copenhaver, 2000, pp. 15-16
5. Ficino, 1996, pp. 167, 168
6. Voss, 2000, pp. 37-39
7. Dyer, 2000
8. Copenhaver, 2000, p. 16
9. Shargel, 2016, pp. 61-85
10. Versluis, 2002, p. 5. The terms emic and etic originated in the study of anthropology and acknowledge that our understanding of another culture can be skewed by our own cultural assumptions. They refer to different standpoints, with the emic perspective giving the insider view from within the culture itself and the etic account being that of an observer and attempts to be 'culturally neutral', limiting any ethnocentric, political, and/or cultural bias or alienation by the observer. The preferred approach combines both perspectives.
11. Versluis, 2002, p. 13
12. Versluis, 2002, p. 13

Chapter 2

1. Goodrick-Clarke, 2008
2. Goodrick-Clarke, p. 3
3. Goodrick-Clarke, p. 19
4. Kingsley, 1993
5. Goodrick-Clarke, p. 19
6. Copenhaver 2000, p. 1
7. Copenhaver 2000, p. 2
8. Copenhaver 2000, p. 1
9. Copenhaver 2000, p. 2
10. Copenhaver 2000, p. 2
11. Copenhaver 2000, p. 3
12. Copenhaver, 2000, p. 3
13. Copenhaver, 2000, p. 47
14. Copenhaver, 2000, p. 16
15. Copenhaver, 2000, p. 41

16. Copenhaver, 2000, p. 18
17. Copenhaver, 2000, p. 35
18. Copenhaver, 2000, p. 6
19. Copenhaver, 2000, pp. 7
20. Copenhaver, 2000, p. 51
21. Moyers & Campbell, 2013
22. Copenhaver, 2000, p. 73
23. Scott, 2000, p. 2
24. Uzdavinys, 2014, p. 306
25. *In Remp.* I.198.15-16
26. Uzdavinys, 2014, p. 306
27. Uzdavinys, 2014, p. 207
28. Uzdavinys, 2014, p. 208
29. Proclus *In Tim*.I.4.32-33
30. Uzdavinys, 2014, p. 306
31. Addey, 2014, pp. 29-30
32. Laboure, 1994
33. Copenhaver, 2000 p. 3
34. Copenhaver, 2000 p. 74
35. Copenhaver, 2000 p. 88
36. Copenhaver, 2000 p. 74
37. Copenhaver, 2000 p. 71
38. Copenhaver, 2000 p. 72
39. Copenhaver, 2000 p. 88
40. Copenhaver, 2000 p. 51
41. Addey, 2014, p. 203
42. Addey, 2014, p. 4
43. Addey, 2014, p. 11
44. Addey, 2014, p. 120
45. Shaw, 2014, pp. 94-95
46. Addey, 2015
47. Copenhaver, 2000 p. 82

Chapter 3

1. Garin, 2000 pp. 59-64
2. Voss, 2006 pp. 71-81
3. Voss, 2006, p. 34
4. Brockbank, p. 40
5. Voss, 2006, p. 34
6. Voss, 2006, p. 35
7. Ficino, 1998, p. 241
8. Voss, 2000, p. 34

9. Voss, 2000, p. 39
10. Ficino, 1998, p. 255
11. Ficino, 1998, pp. 245-247
12. Ficino, 1998, p. 251
13. Voss, 2011, p. 1
14. Allen, 1995, p. 87
15. Voss, 2011, p. 4
16. Voss, 2011, p. 2
17. Garin 2000, p. 74
18. Corbin, 1971
19. Ficino, 1998 p. 251
20. Ficino, 1998 p. 243
21. Ficino, 1998, p. 243
22. Ficino, 1998, p. 243
23. Ficino, 1998, p. 243
24. Ficino, 2016 pp. 46–47
25. Ficino, 1975, p. 43
26. Ficino, 1975, p. 43
27. Ficino, 1996, pp. 64-69
28. Ficino, 1996, p. 65
29. Ficino, 1975 p. 44
30. Voss, 2000, p. 34
31. Ficino, 1975, pp. 35-39
32. Ficino, 1975, p. 36
33. Ficino, 1975, p. 37
34. Ficino, 1975, p. 38
35. There is some inconsistency in the sources as to whether the word sun should be capitalised. I have followed the sources when quoting. However, in this chapter I have preferred capital letters for the initials of all the planets to indicate Ficino's view that he is referring to their spiritual and daemonic personalities rather than their material forms. See Ficino, 1998, p. 247
36. Copenhaver, 2000, p. 40
37. Ficino, 1998, p. 251
38. Ficino, 1998, p. 311
39. Ficino, 1998, p. 311
40. Ficino, 1998, p. 311
41. Ficino, 1998, p. 345
42. Ficino, 1998, p. 345
43. Ficino, 1975, p. 40
44. Ficino, 1996, p. 125
45. Ficino, 1996, p. 125
46. Ficino, 1996, p. 160
47. Voss, 2006, p. 27

48. Voss, 2006, p. 27
49. Ficino, 1998, p. 275
50. Ficino, 1998, p. 275
51. Ficino, 1996, p. 160
52. Corbin, 1971
53. Burckhardt, p. 13
54. Ficino, 1996 pp. 61-63
55. Allen, 1995, p. 79
56. Allen, 1995, p. 81
57. Copenhaver, 2000, p. 90
58. Copenhaver, 2000, pp. 90-91
59. Ficino, 1998, p. 353
60. Young, 2016
61. Ficino, 1998, p. 405

Chapter 4

1. Cornelius, 2009
2. Willis & Curry, pp. 77-86
3. McGilchrist, 2009
4. Jung, 1971
5. McGilchrist, 2009, p. 160
6. Chapman, 2002
7. McGilchrist, 2009
8. McGilchrist, 2009, p. 38
9. McGilchrist, 2009, p. 49
10. McGilchrist, 2009, p. 81
11. McGilchrist, 2009, p. 83
12. McGilchrist, 2009, p. 79
13. McGilchrist, 2009, p. 58
14. Copenhaver, 2000, p. 16
15. McGilchrist, 2009, pp. 50-51
16. McGilchrist, 2009, p. 56
17. McGilchrist, 2009, p. 41
18. McGilchrist, 2009, p. 43
19. McGilchrist, 2009, p. 51
20. McGilchrist, 2009, p. 77
21. McGilchrist, 2009, p. 71
22. McGilchrist, 2009, p. 160
23. McGilchrist, 2009, p. 62
24. McGilchrist, 2009, p. 86
25. Naydler, 2005, Preface
26. Naydler, 2005, Preface
27. McGilchrist, 2009, p. 347

28. McGilchrist, 2009, p. 14
29. Chapman, 2002, p. 12
30. Chapman, 2012
31. Voss, 2006, p. 75
32. McGilchrist, 2009, p. 329
33. Aniela Jaffe says: "It is the answer the Delphic Oracle gave the Lacedemonians when they were planning a war against Athens" 1979: 136. In a letter of November 19, 1960, Jung explains the inscription: "By the way, you seek the enigmatic oracle *Vocatus atque non vocatus deus aderit* in vain in Delphi: it is cut in stone over the door of my house in Kusnacht near Zurich and otherwise found in Erasmus's collection of *Adagia* XVIth cent.. [Jung had acquired a copy of the 1563 edition of Erasmus's *Collectaneas adagiorum*, a compilation of analects from classical authors, when he was 19 years old.] It is a Delphic oracle though. It says: yes, the god will be on the spot, but in what form and to what purpose? I have put the inscription there to remind my patients and myself: *Timor dei initium sapiente* ["The fear of the Lord is the beginning of wisdom."] Here another not less important road begins, not the approach to 'Christianity' but to God himself and this seems to be the ultimate question." 1975: 611
34. Schlamm, 2007, p. 1
35. Willis & Curry, 2004, p. 77
36. Jung, 1964, p. 95
37. Jung, 1971, p. 25
38. Scott, 2000, p. 2
39. Main, 2007, p. 27
40. Main, 2007, p. 28
41. Main, 2007, p. 29
42. Main, 2007, p. 29
43. Main, 2007, p. 32
44. Jung, 1969, p. 353
45. Jung, 1971, p. 22
46. Jung, 1971, p. 357
47. Jung, 1971, p. 357
48. Tyas, 2010, p. 13
49. Cornelius, 2009, pp. 106-204
50. Hyde, 1992, pp. 78-79
51. Hyde relates a story shared by Lindsay Radermacher about her chart for a dead fox. She felt the moment of seeing the fox was significant but could not tell why and could not discern relevant symbolism in the chart. However, when giving a lecture on 'dead' charts she found to her consternation that the symbol came to life and appeared to describe both the audience and the chart. She later found that foxes sometimes pretend to be dead in order to catch their prey.

52. Hyde, 1992, p. 71
53. Hyde, 1992, p. 79
54. Hyde, 1992, p. 143
55. Hyde, 1992, pp. 91-101
56. Shargel 2016 p. 70
57. Cornelius, 2003, pp. 292-296
58. Shargel, 2016, p. 72
59. Shargel, 2016, p. 75
60. Halevi, 1986
61. Fernandez, 1991; Kracke, 1992
62. Tedlock, 2001, p. 191
63. Scott, 2000, p. 2
64. Scott, 2000, p. 9
65. Scott, 2000, p. 12
66. Milne, 2007, p. 7

Part 2

1. Landwehr, 2004, p. 31
2. Ficino, 2002, p. 243
3. 'Arabi, 1976, p. 13
4. Addey, 2015
5. Lachman, 2011, pp. 31 - 33
6. Lachman, 2011, p. 31
7. Copenhaver, 2000, p. 3 v.14
8. Addas, 2016
9. www.ibnarabisociety.org.uk/articles/addas1.html "The… hadith qudsî-s.. whose authenticity Ibn Arabî certifies by virtue of a revelation kashf answers the question about why the world was created: "I was a hidden treasure and I loved to be known; so I created the creatures and made Myself known to them; so they knew Me."
10. Kingsley, 2009, p. 2
11. Lachman, 2015, p. 170
12. Lachman, 2011, p. 111
13. Ficino, 2002, pp. 321-323
14. Saif, 2015, electronic book, pp. 759-765/8121
15. Ficino, 2002, p. 245
16. Rumi, 1978, p. 31
17. There are a number of examples. In his footnote on p. 31 of *Rumi: Poet and Mystic* Nicholson refers to the Mathnawi, explaining that the reed is the Persian reed-flute. "Rumi uses it as a symbol for the soul emptied of self and filled with the Divine spirit. This blessed soul, during its life on Earth, remembers the union with God which it enjoyed in eternity and longs ardently for deliverance from the world where it is a stranger and exile."

18. Arabi', 1998, p. 54
19. Ecclesiastes, 1982, p. 450
20. Rumi, 1978, p. 31
21. Copenhaver, 2000, p. 16
22. McGilchrist, 2009, p. 61
23. Copenhaver, 2000, p. 74 s.12
24. Copenhaver, 2000, p. 16 s.5
25. Copenhaver, 2000, p. 74, s.13
26. Copenhaver, 2000, p. 74 s.12
27. Copenhaver, 2000, p. 82 s.25
28. The passage continues "only the baleful angels remain to mingle with humans, seizing the wretches and driving them to every outrageous crime – war, looting, trickery and all that is contrary to the nature of souls. Then neither will the earth stand firm nor the sea be sailable; stars will not cross heaven nor will the course of the stars stand firm in heaven. Every divine voice will grow mute in enforced silence. The fruits of the earth will rot; the soil will no more be fertile; and the very air will droop in gloomy lethargy."
29. Copenhaver, 2000, p. 47 s. 19
30. Addey, 2015
31. Copenhaver, 2000, pp. 73,74 s.11
32. Addey, 2015
33. The human heart is the physical and subtle centre by virtue of which man is distinguishable from all other creatures. It is each person's 'connection' to their divine, essential reality, which alone can comprehend deep meanings and 'see' the underlying unity of all existence. It is the birth right of all humanity, innate in each of us. An education for man is that which accords the heart its central position and allows it to be the real 'organ' of intelligence, and to govern all other faculties. With this, education returns to its original meaning of 'drawing forth' from within. http://www.beshara.org/principles/talks-and-articles/lectures-and-talks/education-of-the-heartPY.html
34. Arabi, 1998, pp. 39, 40
35. Copenhaver, 2000, p. 16 s.5
36. Copenhaver, 2000, p. 15 s.4
37. Ficino, 2002, p. 195
38. Young, 1982
39. Halevi, 1991, p. 173
40. Halevi connects both the Sun and pride with the Sephira of Tiferet.
41. Kupperman, 2013, p. 45
42. Ficino, 2002, p. 263
43. In the symbolism of the Sema ritual, the semazen's camel's hair hat (sikke) represents the tombstone of the ego; his wide, white skirt represents the ego's shroud. By removing his black cloak, he is spiritually

reborn to the truth. http://www.whirlingdervishes.org/whirlingdervish-es.htm

44. Ficino, 2002, p. 295
45. http://www.ibnarabisociety.org.uk/articles/union_ibnarabi.html Hadith kudsi or saying of the Prophet, interpreted by Ibn 'Arabi as the death of the ego.
46. Rumi, 1978, pp. 182, 183
47. The labyrinth coordinator had some intriguing observations taken from the visits of primary school children to the labyrinth. She asked them what the image on the floor reminded them of. One saw the image as a picture of the brain. This picks up the twists and turns in the path. It is these twists and turns that seem to me to be analogous to our lives and to the challenges in the journey of the soul. These are further imaged in the apparent movement of the moveable stars (the planets) direct and retrograde, the governors or ousiarches of the story. Another child thought the labyrinth looked like a womb. Again, I can see that the central enclosure and the circuits surrounding it, offering both sustenance and an escape, is very like a womb. The image conjures up the lines in Rumi's poem *The Soul of the World*: "I was with Him then as a child in the womb". It is an image of love, safety, nourishment and protection. For me this also reminded me of an occasion when I visited the Beshara School at Chisholme for zikr. When we came out, the night was clear. The milky way was clearly visible. The stars seemed to stretch down towards us as though we ourselves were each of us the child in that cosmic womb.

Part 3

1. Addas, 2016
2. Copenhaver, 2000, p. 3 s. 12
3. Copenhaver, 2000, p. 3 s.14
4. Rumi, 1978, p. 36
5. Copenhaver, 2000, p. 35 s.23
6. The reference comes from an unpublished Beshara paper titled "The Five Things", probably written by Bulent Rauf.
7. Rumi, 1978, p. 122
8. Kupperman, 2013, p. 47
9. Ficino, 2002, p. 247
10. Heart chakra
11. Ficino, 2002, p. 195
12. 'Arabi, n.d., p. 16
13. Rumi, 1978, pp. 122-123
14. Rumi, 1982, p. 5
15. Copenhaver, 2000, p. 47 s.18

16. Copenhaver, 2000, p. 42
17. Copenhaver, 2000, p. 48
18. Copenhaver, 2000, p. 47 s.19
19. Copenhaver, 2000, p. 16 s.5
20. Rumi, 1978, p. 121
21. 'Arabi, 1978, pp. 67 vs 13-15
22. 'Arabi, 1998, p. 40
23. Copenhaver, 2000, p. 82 s.25
24. Copenhaver, 2000, p. 71 s.8
25. Copenhaver, 2000, p. 85
26. Copenhaver, 2000, p. 34 s.18
27. Copenhaver, 2000, p. 34 s.19
28. Lee, 2016
29. Rumi, 1978, pp. 182-3